1. Die Festung Meissenburg. 2. das Peters Thor. 3. S. Peters Kirch. 4. Proviant Haus 5. Bosens Garten. 6. S. Thomas Kirch. 7. das Gewand=Haus. 8. die Barfüsser oder tcute Kirch. 9. das Rath=Haus thürnl. 10. die Pauliner Kirch u. Collegium. 11. das Grim=nische Thor. 12. die S. Nicolaus Kirch. 13. S. Johanns od' Begräbnis Kirch. 14. das Reiche Spittal. 15. das Zucht u. Waisen=Haus.

JOHANN SEBASTIAN BACH

His Life in Pictures and Documents

HANS CONRAD FISCHER

Hänssler – Illustrated Book

Order No.: 393.438
ISBN 3-7751-3438-7

English translation: Silvia Lutz
Editors: Christopher Pipe
and Tim Dowley

Redesigned edition: 2000

Layout: Peter Wyart,
Three's Company, London

Frontispiece: Portrait of J.S. Bach

Printed in Italy by G. Canale & C. S.p.A. - Turin

Worldwide coedition organized and
produced by
Angus Hudson Ltd,
Concorde House, Grenville Place,
Mill Hill, London NW7 3SA, England
tel (+44) 020 8959 3668
fax (+44) 020 8959 3678

Page 2: Johann Sebastian Bach. Oil painting by Elias Gottlob Haussmann, 1746.

Contents

Preface

The reader at the beginning of the 21st century is 'enlightened.' He finds himself at a late (and perhaps even final) stage of a development in the European history of ideas whose roots reach back far beyond Johann Sebastian Bach's time. In the period between Bach's birth and his death, this development changed the Western world decisively. In historical terms it is called the Enlightenment, but we soon begin to wonder if we should regard this enlightenment with the same naive belief in progress, even euphoria, as our ancestors did. The achievements of technology, civilization and politics since the 18th century have radically changed human thinking and our worldview. They have made the material side of human life much easier. However, there are an increasing number of people who are convinced that the development of human thought since Bach's day, the immense accumulation of intellectual knowledge, has not been an undisputed progress of history, since our souls have not grown accordingly. The caricature of man with a huge head sitting on a minuscule body with a stunted heart has become reality. We cannot ignore this reality. It threatens to suffocate us.

In Johann Sebastian Bach's time, this distortion was unknown. When we listen to his music today, many of us are filled with an inner peace which is in complete contrast to the restlessness, doubts and fears of our own existence. We long for the harmony we feel in this music, but we no longer experience this harmony. Have we become prisoners, even

exiles, of our knowledge and our doubts? We have succeeded in doubling our life expectancy since Bach's days, but have our souls become diseased? Nowadays, Johann Sebastian Bach's music is used as therapy in hospitals, and not only for calming those suffering from nervous diseases. This music, and the historic personality of its composer, communicate something from another age to today's listener. The distance of three centuries somehow transfigures Bach's music. Everything about Bach and his music seems to be extraordinary; but this idea is a profound error which is carried on from generation to generation. Since the beginning of the 19th century, when people began to rediscover the more or less forgotten Cantor of St. Thomas's in Leipzig, each generation has added to the sentimentalising of Bach's image.

We are 'enlightened.' We have lost the humility – some may say the naiveté – of faith which governed Johann Sebastian Bach's daily life and music. His contemporaries sang, played and listened to his compositions with the same humility and faith. Instead of a concert hall, the radio, the stereo system, records, cassettes, CDs, the TV – all the means of listening to music today – there was one firmly rooted centre for performing music: the church. Even secular music promoted by the royal courts and capitals, which were very numerous at Bach's time in Germany, was firmly anchored in the Christian faith. The same was true of popular music. Within his everyday life, Johann

Sebastian Bach created music for his contemporaries' everyday lives. At the centre of this everyday life were prayer and worship. Bach did not worry whether posterity would appreciate his creative work.

This attitude, mentioned by Albert Schweitzer in his important biography at the beginning of the 20th century, has been confirmed with meticulousness by Bach experts in recent decades. Those who want to approach the phenomenon of Johann Sebastian Bach must start from the strong faith of Bach's soul, whether or not the reader shares this faith. We should not try to explain the unexplainable or analyse the metaphysical basis of Bach's music. We must be content with the old wisdom that there are things in heaven and earth that cannot be grasped by our intellect. One of these things is the way that an organist, choirmaster and court composer from the 18th century called J.S. Bach fulfilled his daily musical duties, argued with town councils, lived, loved and composed music. Three letters are written at the end of many of his music manuscripts: 'SDG' – *Soli Deo Gloria*: for God's glory alone.

Bach's music has engrossed generations of scholars and challenged generations of musicians to analyse its forms and interpretation, yet it is just as inexplicable as the phenomenon of Johann Sebastian Bach himself. It can only be admired or rejected, according to one's own viewpoint in time and history. Much research into Bach's music and compositional techniques is good, and some is excellent; the author does not want to add another attempt but to document Johann Sebastian Bach's life, give an overview of the facts, times and living conditions in which Bach's artistic work came into being. The present work will add a few thoughts to today's understanding of Bach, but above all it will illustrate. It is for the reader to come to conclusions about Bach's life and work; the text and pictures of this book are intended to help in this.

The texts of Bach and his contemporaries which are quoted in what follows are taken from the supplementary volumes of the *Neue Ausgabe Sämtlicher Werke* (New Edition of the Complete Works) of Johann Sebastian Bach, published jointly by Bärenreiter and VEB Deutscher Verlag für Musik.

Background and Childhood

Bach's native town of Eisenach is dominated by the Wartburg. Looking down from this castle we see a peaceful little town lying in the midst of the wide Thuringian countryside, with its forests and hills. To the west and to the south, there are dark green fir forests and bright green deciduous forests, shimmering with thousands of colours in autumn. Many of these great old trees may even have stood there when Frederick, Electoral Prince of Saxony, called 'the Wise' by posterity, pretended to kidnap the Augustinian monk Martin Luther on his way home from Worms to Wittenberg and had him taken to the Wartburg to save him from being executed as a heretic. On 10 December 1520, on a cold winter's morning, surrounded by a number of enthusiastic supporters and students, Luther threw into the fire the papal letter of excommunication which had been issued against him. One year later, at the Imperial Diet at Worms in 1521, Emperor Charles V proclaimed Luther an outlaw. A papal letter of excommunication and outlawry in the Emperor's name – who would imagine things like that if we had not the portrait painted by Luther's relation Lucas Cranach the Elder in 1521? This portrait shows the reformer as 'Sir George', with long hair and a full beard. World-shaking events in the history of religion had been concealed for two short years behind a beard, old trees and the walls of the Wartburg.

If we visit Bach's native town, we immediately meet that great personality of German and European history without whom Johann Sebastian Bach's life's work would be inconceivable: Martin Luther. As a young boy, Luther had lived in Eisenach for some time and attended the parish school of St. George's. Years later, he spoke of his 'dear Eisenach' – words of affection he did not have for any other town. Martin Luther, the Reformation and the home of the Bach family in Thuringia are inseparable. In 1517, that is 168 years before Johann Sebastian Bach was born, Luther nailed his 95 Theses to the castle church of Wittenberg, triggering the Reformation. Because of their Lutheran belief, Bach's ancestors had to leave their home in Hungary. In Thuringia, the centre of the Reformation, they found a new home. From the first known ancestor down to Johann Sebastian Bach and his entire life-work, the destiny of the Bach family is closely linked with Martin Luther.

In a room in the Wartburg, today called 'Luther's Room,' Luther began translating the Bible which formed the spiritual basis of the New High German language. The Bible was also the basis of the life work of the musician Johann Sebastian Bach, who was born on March 21, 1685, below this same Wartburg. *I purchased these excellent German writings by the late Dr M. Luther at an auction* wrote the 57-year-old Bach, recording additions to his library of Luther's works in September 1742. About a third of Bach's library of theological books consisted of Martin Luther's works and commentaries on them – 21 thick folio volumes. Luther's influence can be detected everywhere in Bach's life and work.

An evangelical Lutheran Christian, Bach considered Martin Luther to be the founder of his church. For Christians today, Luther was the great personality at the beginning of modern times who eloquently opposed the profaning of the gospel by secular power politics, by betrayal and by criminal acts. In doing so, Luther changed the path of history. But it is often forgotten that Luther was not only a reformer but also one of the great linguistic phenomena of history. He listened to what people really said as few had done before. This is why his Bible text and hymns could so easily be set to music and sung, as we see in Bach's works. The close relationship to music inspired by the sensitivity the linguist Luther had for music seems like the beginning of a dialogue with Johann Sebastian Bach, despite the one and a half centuries separating him from Bach's birth. On the other hand, the musician Bach had a similarly close and sensitive relationship with words. Is it geographical coincidence, is it merely down to the vagaries of world history, that Bach was born below the very same castle where the eloquent 'Sir George' sat over the texts of the gospel?

Johann Sebastian Bach himself gave information about his ancestors in Thuringia in his genealogy *Origin of the Musical Bach Family*, written in 1735. This genealogy has been preserved in a copy by Bach's granddaughter Anna Carolina Philippina, with supplements by her father, Carl Philipp Emanuel, Johann Sebastian's second son. On seventeen hand-written pages, we can read the dates and occupations of Bach's ancestors and descendants. We see the development of the musical Bach family over a period of two centuries before reaching its climax in Johann Sebastian and branching out in the history of European music through his sons.

The gaps in the following text mark where Bach's genealogical knowledge and memory failed.

1. Martin Luther. Oil painting by Lucas Cranach the Elder, 1526.

2. Martin Luther as 'Sir George'. Oil painting by Lucas Cranach the Elder, 1521.

1

Origin of the Musical Bach Family

No. 1. Vitus Bach, a baker in Hungary. He had to leave Hungary in the 16th century because of his Lutheran religion. After selling as much of his property as possible, he moved to Germany; since he found security and was not persecuted because of his Lutheran belief in Thuringia, he settled at Wechmar near Gotha and continued to work as a baker. He loved playing his cittern [a kind of lute]. He even took the instrument to the mill and played it while grinding the corn. (A pretty sound they must have made together! He really learned to keep time.) That was the beginning of music in his family and in his children. He died on   .

No. 2. Johannes Bach, the son of the former, first worked as a baker. But because he had a special love for music, he served his apprenticeship with the Stadtpfeifer [wind players] at Gotha. At that time, the old castle of Grimmenstein had not yet been destroyed, and his master lived in the tower of the castle, as was customary for men of his position. He continued working for the Stadtpfeifer even after completing his apprenticeship; but after the destruction of the castle (it was destroyed in the year 15   ) and since his father Veit had died in the meantime, he moved to Wechmar where he married the spinster Anna Schmied, the daughter of an inn-keeper at Wechmar, and took over his father's property. After his return to Wechmar he was called several times to Gotha, Arnstadt, Erfurt, Eisenach, Schmalkalden and Suhl to assist the musicians of these towns. He died in 1626 of a contagion raging at the time. After his death his wife lived for nine more years as a widow and died in 1635.

No. 3. His brother   Bach was a carpet maker and had three sons who learned to make music. The Earl of Schwartzburg-Arnstadt who was in power at the time sent them to Italy to study music at his expense. The youngest of these three brothers had an accident and lost his eyesight. He was called 'blind Jonas.' Many bizarre stories have been told about this man's adventures. Since he died without marrying, all the descendants in the genealogy by the name of Bach descend from his two brothers, who lived at Mechterstädt (situated between Eisenach and Gotha) and in the surrounding villages. Kapellmeister [director of music] Johann Ludwig Bach who died in 1730 at Meinungen, and whose late father, Jacob Bach, had been choirmaster at Ruhl were descendants of this family; as well as Stephan Bach, former choirmaster at the cathedral in Brunswick, who died many years ago (his brother   Bach was a priest at Lähnstädt, near Weimar). This lineage is said to include the names of some inhabitants, among them the family of Seebach, particularly in Opfershausen; but it is not known for certain if these really are descendants of this line.

No. 4. Johannes Bach. He was the eldest son of Hans Bach **(2)** and was born at Wechmar on 26 November 1604. Since he accompanied his father, Hans Bach, whenever he was called to the towns mentioned above, the old Stadtpfeifer at Suhl, Hoffmann, persuaded Hans Bach to apprentice his son to him. His father agreed. He stayed at Suhl for five years as an apprentice and two years as a journeyman. Then he moved to Schweinfurt, where he became an organist. In the year 1635, he was called to Erfurt as director of the council's musicians. He accepted this call; after many years he was given the organist's post at the Prediger-Kirche [church]. He died in 1673. He married twice. His first wife was spinster Barbara Hoffmann, the daughter of his dear master. By her he fathered a son who was stillborn. His wife died half an hour after giving birth to the dead child. Later he married spinster Hedewig Lämmerhirt, the daughter of Mr Valentin Lämmerhirt's relative at Erfurt. By her he fathered three sons **(7, 8** and **9)**.

No. 5. Christoph Bach, the second son of Hans Bach **(2)** was also born at Wechmar in the year 1613, on April 19. He also studied instrumental music. At first he served the prince at the court in Weimar; later he was in service of the town musicians at Erfurt and

later at Arnstadt, where he died on 12 September 1661. He was married to spinster Maria Magdalena Grabler, who was born at Prettin in Saxony, and fathered the three sons listed as **10**, **11** and **12** by his wife. She died 24 days after the death of her late husband Christoph on 6 October 1661 at Arnstadt.

No. 6. Heinrich Bach, the third son of Hans Bach **(2)** served in the town musicians of Arnstadt as did his brother Christoph. He also worked as town organist. He was born at Wechmar in the year 1615, on December 16. He died in 1692 at Arnstadt. He was married to spinster Eva Hoffmann from Suhl, presumably a sister of Barbara Hoffmann **(4)**.

No. 7. Christian Bach, the eldest son of Johann Bach **(4)**. He was born at Erfurt in 1640. He died there as director of the town's musicians in 1682. His two sons are listed as nos. **16** and **17**.

No. 8. Joh. Egidius Bach, the other son of Johann Bach **(4)** was born at Erfurt in 1645. He was director of the town's musicians and organist of St. Michael's and died there in the year 1717. His two sons are listed as nos. **18** and **19**.

No. 9. Johann Nicolaus Bach, the third son of Johann Bach **(4)**, was born in 1653 and grew up at Erfurt. He was very good on the viole da gamba and belonged to the Town Compagnie. He died of the plague in 1682 and had one son, Joh. Nicolaus **(20)**.

No. 10. Georg Christoph Bach. He was the first-born son of Christoph Bach **(5)**. He was born on September 6, 1642. He was appointed choirmaster at Schweinfurt and died there in the year 16 . His sons are listed under no. **21**.

No. 11. Johann Ambrosius Bach, the second son of Christoph Bach **(5)**. He was court and town musician at Eisenach. He was born at Erfurt in the year 1645, on February 22. He died at Eisenach in the year 1695. He was married to spinster Elisabeth Lämmerhirt, the spinster daughter of a relation of Valentin Lämmerhirt at Erfurt; he fathered eight children by his wife: six sons and two daughters. Three of their sons and their youngest daughter died unmarried. Three sons and their eldest daughter survived their parents and married. They are listed as nos. **22**, **23** and **24**.

No. 12. Johann Christoph Bach, the twin brother of Ambrosius **(11)** and Christoph Bach's third son, was court and town musician at Arnstadt. With spinster Martha Elisabeth Eisentraut, the virgin daughter of Franz Eisentraut, the verger of Ohrdruf, he fathered the sons listed as nos. **25** and **26**.

No. 13. Johann Christoph Bach, the first son of Heinrich Bach **(6)** was born at Arnstadt in the year   . He died at Eisenach as court and town organist in 1703. He was a gifted composer. By his wife, Mrs   née Wiedemann, the eldest daughter of Mr Wiedemann, town clerk at Arnstadt, he fathered the four sons listed as nos. **27**, **28**, **29** and **30**.

No. 14. Johann Michael Bach, another son of Heinrich Bach **(6)** was also born at Arnstadt in the year   . He was town clerk and organist at Gehren. Like his elder brother, he was a talented composer. When he died, he left a widow, the second daughter of Mr. Wiedemann, the town clerk of Arnstadt, and four unmarried daughters, but no son.

No. 15. Johann Günther Bach, the third son of Heinrich Bach **(6)** was an assistant to his father. He was a good musician and a skilful builder of various new musical instruments. He died in the year 16   without leaving a male heir.

No. 16. Johann Jacob Bach, the eldest son of Johann Christian Bach **(7)**, was born at Erfurt in 1668. He worked for Johann Ambrosius Bach as a caretaker and died unmarried at Eisenach in 1692.

No. 17. Johann Christoph Bach, the second son of Johann Christian Bach **(7)**. He was born at Erfurt in 1673. He worked as a choirmaster at Gehren and died in the year 1727. His children are listed as nos. **31**, **32** and **33**.

No. 18. Joh. Bernhard Bach, the eldest son of Johann Egidius Bach **(8)** was born in 1676 at Erfurt. Now, in the year 1735, he is still alive and works as a chamber musician and as an organist at Eisenach. He succeeded Johann Christ. Bach **(13)**. His only son is listed as no. **34**.

No. 19. Joh. Christoph Bach, the second son of Johann Egidius Bach **(8)**, was born at Erfurt in 1685. He is director of the town's musicians at Erfurt. His sons are listed as nos. **35**, **36** and **37**.

No. 20. Joh. Nicolaus Bach, a son of Joh. Nic.

3. The Wartburg.

Bach **(9)**, became a surgeon and lives ten miles from Königsberg in Prussia, in   but has a house full of children.

No. 21. Joh. Valentin Bach, a son of Georg Christoph Bach **(10)**. His brothers are:

No. 22. Joh. Christoph Bach, the eldest son of Joh. Ambrosius Bach **(11)**. He was born on in the year 167   . He died at Ohrdruf as an organist and school teacher in 17

No. 23. Joh. Jacob Bach, the second son of Joh. Ambrosius Bach **(11)**. He was born at Eisenach in 1682. He learned to be a Stadtpfeifer and became an apprentice to his late father's successor, Heinrich Halle; after some years, in 1704, he entered the service of the Swedish army as an oboist. He was lucky enough to reach the Turkish town of Bender with King Charles XII after the unhappy battle of Pultava. He had stayed with the king for eight or nine years and retired as royal chamber and court musician in Stockholm one year before the king returned. There he died in the year 17   , without issue.

No. 24. Joh. Sebastian Bach. The youngest son of Joh. Ambrosius Bach, born at Eisenach on 21 March, 1685. He became (1) court musician at Weimar to Duke Herzog Johann Ernst in 1703, (2) organist at the Neukirche, Arnstadt, in 1704, (3) organist at St. Blasius's, Mühlhausen, in 1707, (4) chamber and court organist at Weimar in 1708, (5) as well as concert master at the same court in 1714. (6) Kapellmeister and director of the chamber musicians at the royal court of Anhalt Cöthen in 1717. (7) He was called to Leipzig in 1723 to become director of the choir and choirmaster at the Thomas school, where he still

4. Luther's Room at the Wartburg.

5. Title page of Luther's version of the Bible, with a note that this copy belonged to Bach, dated 1733. This copy of the three volumes of the Bible edited by the Wittenberg theologian Abraham Calov in 1681 is the only book of Bach's library which has been discovered so far. In this book, many notes and comments by Bach can be found.

J. N. J.

Die Heilige Bibel

nach S. Herrn D. MARTINI LUTHERI
Deutscher Dolmetschung/ und Erklärung/
vermöge des Heil. Geistes/
im Grund=Text/
Richtiger Anleitung der Cohærentz,
Und der gantzen Handlung eines jeglichen Texts/
Auch Vergleichung der gleichlautenden Sprüche/ enthaltenen
eigenen Sinn und Meinung/
Nechst ordentlicher Eintheilung eines jeden Buches und Capitels/
und Erwegung der nachdrücklichen Wort/ und Redens=Art
in der Heil. Sprache/
sonderlich aber
Der Evangelischen allein seligmachenden Warheit/
gründ= und deutlich erörtert/
und mit Anführung
Herrn LUTHERI deutschen/ und verdeutschten Schrifften/
also abgefasset/
daß der eigentliche Buchstäbliche Verstand/
und gutes Theils auch
der heilsame Gebrauch der Heil. Schrifft
fürgestellet ist/
Mit grossem Fleiß/ und Kosten ausgearbeitet/
und verfasset/
von

D. ABRAHAM CALOVIO,

Im Jahr Christi cIꝺ Iꝺc XXCI.
welches ist das *1681*
5681ste Jahr/ von Erschaffung der Welt.
Zu Wittenberg/
Nicht uns HERR/ nicht uns/ sondern deinem Namen gib Ehre/
umb deiner Gnade und Warheit!

Gedruckt in Wittenberg/ bey Christian Schrödtern/ der Univ. Buchdr.

lives, by God's grace, and works as Kapellmeister of Weissenfels and Cöthen. His descendants are as follows:

No. 25. Joh. Ernst Bach. the first son of Joh. Christoph Bach **(12)**. He was born in 1683, on 5 August. He is organist at the Oberkirche, Arnstadt. His children are mentioned in nos.

No. 26. Joh. Christoph Bach, the second son of Joh. Christoph Bach. He lives at Plankenhayn and earns his living as a grocer. He is married, but has no heirs. He was born on 12 September 1689.

No. 27. Joh. Nicolaus Bach. The eldest of all the living Bachs, the eldest son of Joh. Christoph Bach **(13)**. He is organist both at the university church and at the Stadtkirche, Jena.

No. 28. Joh. Christoph Bach, the second son of Joh. Christoph Bach **(13)**. He also loves music, but never earned his living by playing music. He rather enjoys travelling.

No. 29. Joh. Friedrich Bach, was the third son of Joh. Christoph Bach **(13)**. He died in 172 after having succeeded J.S. Bach as organist of St. Blasius's, Mühlhausen. He had no heirs.

No. 30. Joh. Michael Bach, the fourth son of Johann Christoph Bach **(13)**. He learned the art of organ-building, but travelled to northern countries and never returned, so there is no information available about him.

No. 31. Joh. Samuel Bach, the eldest son of J.C. Bach **(17)**; he died very young and was a musician at Sondershausen.

No. 32. Joh. Christian Bach, the second son of J. Ch. Bach **(17)**; he was a musician, too, and died very young at Sondershausen.

No. 33. Joh. Günther Bach, the third son of J.C. Bach **(17)**, is a capable tenor and is still a school teacher for the members of the Merchants' Guild, Erfurt.

No. 34. Joh. Ernst Bach, the only son of Joh. Bernh. Bach **(18)**. He was born in 1722. Besides his studies, he will also make music.

No. 35. Joh. Friedrich Bach, the eldest son of J.C. Bach **(19)**, is a schoolmaster at Andisleben.

No. 36. Joh. Egidius Bach, another son of J.C. Bach **(19)**, is a schoolmaster at Großenmunra.

No. 37. Wilhelm Hieronymus Bach, the third son of J.C. Bach **(19)**.

No. 38. Joh. Lorenz Bach, the eldest son of Joh. Valent. Bach **(21)**. He is organist at

Lahme in Franconia.

No. 39. Joh. Elias Bach, the second son of J. Valent., choirmaster at Schweinfurt.

No. 40. Tobias Friedrich Bach, the eldest son of Joh. Christoph Bach **(22)**, is choirmaster at Udestädt, not far from Erfurt. He was born in 1695.

No. 41. Joh. Bernhard Bach, the second son of J.C. Bach **(22)** just mentioned. He succeeded his late father as organist at Ohrdruf. He was born in 1691.

No. 42. Joh. Christoph Bach, the third son of J.C. Bach **(22)**, is choirmaster and school teacher at Ohrdruf, born in 1   .

No. 43. Joh. Heinrich Bach, the fourth son of J.C. Bach **(22)**. He is in the service of the Count of Hohenlohe as a musician and choirmaster at Oehringen. He was born in 17   .

No. 44. Joh. Andreas Bach, the fifth son of J.C. Bach **(22)**, is an oboist in military service with the Prince of Gotha. He was born in 17   .

No. 45. Wilhelm Friedemann Bach, the eldest son of Joh. Seb. Bach **(24)**. He is working as organist at the Sophienkirche, Dresden. He was born on 22 November 1710.

No. 46. Carl Philipp Emanuel Bach, the second son of Joh. Seb. Bach **(24)**. He lives in Frankfurt-an-der-Oder as a student and studies the piano. He was born on 14 March 1714.

No. 47. Joh. Gottfried Bernhard Bach, the third son of Joh. Seb. Bach **(24)**. He is organist at St. Mary's, also known as the Oberkirche, Mühlhausen. He was born on 11 May 1715.

No. 48. Gottfried Heinrich Bach, the fourth son of Joh. Seb. Bach **(24)**. He was born on 26 February 1724, and he has an inclination for music, particularly the piano.

No. 49. Joh. Christoph Friedrich Bach, the fifth son of Joh. Seb. Bach **(24)**. He was born on 21 June 1732.

No. 50. Joh. Christian Bach, the sixth son of Joh. Seb. Bach **(24)**. He was born on September 5, 1735.

No. 51. Joh. Christoph Bach, the eldest son of Joh. Nicolaus Bach **(27)**.

No. 52.   Bach, the second son of Joh. Nic. Bach **(27)**.

No. 53. Joh. Heinrich Bach, the only son of Joh. Christoph Bach **(28)**. He is a good pianist in the year 173   .

6. Johann Ambrosius Bach (1645-1695). Oil painting, attributed to Johann David Herlicius.

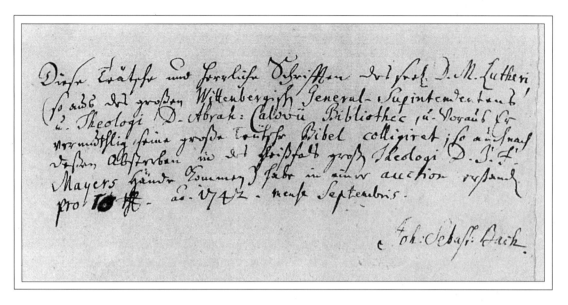

7. Receipt from a book auction for buying Luther's writings, signed by Bach, in September 1742.

If we look at this genealogy comprising 53 Bachs, Johann Sebastian Bach **(24)** is found in the middle of a family dynasty of musicians which is unique in the entire history of music. The baker Vitus Bach who loved playing the lute had some seventy descendants who earned their living as musicians. This lineage was continued by Johann Sebastian Bach and his sons. More than sixty of them remained in central Germany. The Bachs had left their mark on music in Thuringia for generations before Johann Sebastian Bach was born in March 1685. Many of Bach's ancestors were composers, as were most of the organists and choirmasters at the time. A lot of their compositions are still extant – some of them works of remarkable originality. They show how deeply the young Johann Sebastian was rooted in the musical tradition of his family. Any music-lover today can convince himself of the compositional talents of Bach's two uncles, Johann Christoph and Johann Michael. Johann Christoph Bach, 1642–1703, worked as court and town organist at Eisenach. Johann Sebastian often listened to his music as a boy. Johann Michael Bach, 1648-1694, was town clerk and organist in the little town of Gehren, 60 miles or so from Eisenach in the Thuringian Forest. Bach later married the youngest of his uncle's four daughters, his cousin Maria Barbara.

The development of the widely-branching Bach family cannot be separated from musical life in Thuringia. Anyone who travels through this countryside, for example on a peaceful snowy winter's day, can still hear the music. Thuringia was an important region for German, and for European, civilization. Nature and culture worked together in this region; their spiritual correspondence can still be experienced. In 1620, the Thuringian pastor and composer Michael Altenburg described the musical life of his homeland as follows: *Just consider the active music life in every village and town. There is hardly a village in Thuringia where music, both instrumental and vocal, is not in full swing. If there is no organ, vocal music is accompanied by at least five or six violins, which has never been seen before.*

Johann Sebastian Bach's family chronicle shows how general musicality and the widespread popularity of music paved the way for

8. Eisenach.

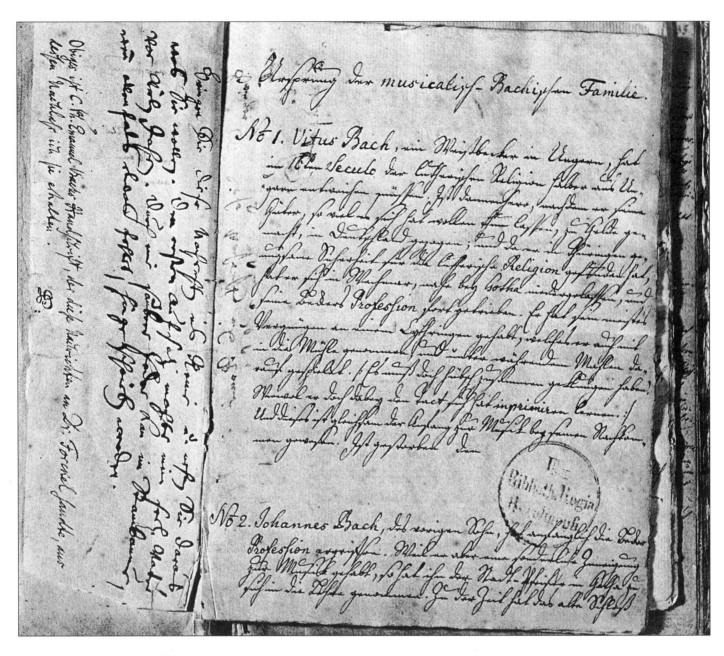

9. 'Origin of the Musical Bach Family', title page. Copy by Anna Carolina Philippina Bach, c. 1775.

the Bachs to improve their income generation after generation by making music. At the beginning of the dynasty, there was the baker Vitus Bach who played the lute just for pleasure and as a way of passing the time. He was succeeded by Stadtpfeifers, as wind players were called at the time, by a player of the viola da gamba, by a musical instrument maker, and by all kinds of town musicians. Bachs became organists and choirmasters, they advanced to become directors of orchestras and finally made it to court musicians, concert and court Kapellmeisters (directors of royal orchestras) and even celebrated court composers. A musical evolution can be observed in this family, reaching its climax in Johann Sebastian and his sons.

Once a year, the members of the Bach family met, usually at Erfurt. At these meetings, they made music, shared the latest family news and discussed their experiences at work and their careers. Musical jobs and posts were shared out among other members of the family, as far as the authorities agreed. The records say that the Bachs were extraordinarily fond of singing at their family meetings. They are said to have sung both their praises to God Almighty and their praises of the pleasures of life with some hearty quodlibet.

Johann Ambrosius, Johann Sebastian's father, moved from Erfurt to Eisenach in 1671, a decade and a half before Bach was born. At Eisenach, he found a job as court and town musician. His wife, Elisabeth, née Lämmerhirt, came from a Thuringian family of manual workers; her father was a furrier at Erfurt. Four of the eight children survived their parents, three sons and one daughter. The youngest son was named Johann Sebastian.

The house in which Bach was born no longer stands. According to historical sources, it must have been like one of those modest town houses which can still be seen in the old town centre. Today's 'Bach's House' at the Frauenplan is a museum which was established in one of the old houses of Eisenach in 1910.

We do not know much about Bach's childhood. From 1693, when he was eight years old, until 1695, when he reached the age of 10, he attended the Latin School in town – the same school that Martin Luther had attended two centuries earlier. Bach's mother died when Johann Sebastian was nine years old. One year later, he lost his father. At the age of 10, Bach was an orphan. This early experience of loss influenced his sense of family all his life.

Youth and First Years

The eldest of Johann Sebastian Bach's brothers, Johann Christoph, was 24 when their father died. He lived in the little Thuringian town of Ohrdruf, a royal seat, where he worked as organist and schoolmaster. Johann Christoph took in the young orphan Johann Sebastian. In the school register of the Lyceum (grammar school) at Ohrdruf, Johann Sebastian Bach is recorded to have attended school from July 20, 1696 to March 15, 1700. During these years, he was taught music by his elder brother. He was presumably called to assist at the organ of St. Michael's, where Johann Christoph worked. Apart from sentimental legends, we have little information about young Johann Sebastian's years at Ohrdruf. Another record in the school register tells of the fifteen-year-old boy moving to Lüneburg.

Johann Christoph's family had increased in number because of his own children. Besides, young Johann Sebastian had to learn to live on his own. So they looked for another home for him. On account of his beautiful voice, he was accepted at the Lyceum of St. Michael's monastery, Lüneburg. Records by the choirmaster of St. Michael's church imply that Bach sang treble in the Lüneburg choir. A note about the 'Matins money' he received survives. The so-called 'Matins pupils' were selected from among the pupils to sing in the school choir. They received free board and lodging, monthly 'Matins money' and free teaching by the monastery. When Johann Sebastian's voice broke, he continued his studies and served as a violinist in the orchestra. At Lüneburg, young Bach came to know a number of the most important works of German sacred music, as well as compositions by Italian masters. Several times, he went to Hamburg to listen to the organist Johann Adam Reincken who worked at the Katharinenkirche. Reincken, who reached the biblical age of 99 years, was well known all over Germany for his numerous powerful choral preludes on the organ.

The free city of Hamburg was the most important commercial metropolis in northern Germany. Hamburg's harbour connected central and northern Germany with the ocean and, thus, with the world. At the same time, Hamburg enjoyed a good reputation for music in Germany, particularly because of its opera. We can assume that young Bach came to know the opera during his stays in Hamburg. In the necrology about his father that Bach's son, Carl Philipp Emanuel, and Bach's student, Johann Friedrich Agricola, wrote four years after Bach's death in 1754, we read that during those years young Bach had been given the opportunity *to become acquainted with the French style of music by listening often to an orchestra famous at the time, employed by the Duke of Celle, and which for the major part consisted of French musicians.* Duke Georg Wilhelm of Braunschweig-Lüneburg, who resided at Celle, was a passionate admirer of French and Italian music. He was married to a French wife whose spirit and beauty were highly praised. Due to her influence, the

10. Erfurt at the time of the Reformation. Oil painting.

orchestra at the ducal court of Celle consisted predominantly of French musicians.

Seen from a historical distance, the ups and downs of Bach's life seem to have turned out well for his artistic work despite some difficulties. Not only did he come from a unique family of musicians, but he also became acquainted with some great masters of the organ at a very young age, particularly Reincken and Georg Böhm, one of Reincken's students, who worked at St. John's, Lüneburg. Very soon Bach became acquainted with famous composers and interpreters of court music of his time, which was influenced by Italian and French music. Bach's musical development had a stable and broad foundation.

After leaving the grammar school at Lüneburg, 18-year-old Johann Sebastian Bach found a job as 'lackey and violinist' in the private orchestra of Johann Ernst, younger brother of the duke of Saxe-Weimar, in March 1703. Today, we cannot hear the name of Weimar without thinking of that glorious period of classic German poetry known by that name. A century before that period, the young Bach came to a Weimar which did not boast the court society of Goethe's time, with their sense of art, nor did the world of literature look to this town. The walls of Weimar castle, which burnt down to its foundations in 1774, were surrounded by a provincial capital. Even in 1785, the poet Johann Gottfried Herder called it *something between a royal capital and a village*. This was 82 years after Bach first started to work there. At the transition from the 17th to the 18th century, Weimar was situated near Erfurt both geographically and spiritually and totally overshadowed by that city's great past. When Martin Luther was a student there, Erfurt had been one of Europe's most important universities, and humanism had found much support there for some time. During the Reformation there had been particularly fierce arguments in Erfurt's numerous churches. The neighbouring town of Weimar had slept undisturbed near this active scene of German history. Weimar's dukes tried to change all this. They were filled with the same cultural ambition as many other rulers of German states in the 18th century. Their ambition particularly focused upon music. This will be dealt with in detail in our description of Bach's life. Bach's acquaintance with the court of Weimar did not last long, and the first time he took an active part in court music did not last long. Only a few months later, Johann Sebastian Bach left Weimar again.

While at Lüneburg, he did his best to get an appointment as organist at Arnstadt. His efforts were supported by his relations at Arnstadt. In July 1703, he received an invitation from Arnstadt *to try out the new organ in the new church*, as it was put in a statement of costs for testing the organ built by Johann Friedrich Wender. A few weeks later, on August 14, 1703, the 18-year-old Johann Sebastian Bach was handed the certificate of appointment for the post of organist at the Neuekirche. His salary, 50 gulden a year and 30 thaler *for board and lodging* was very high for a young man of his age. This sum reflected the enthusiasm of the citizens of Arnstadt for his trial performance and Bach's relationship with the mayor. Later quarrels with the church authorities of Arnstadt overshadowed the favourable constellation that this new post meant for young Bach. The new Wender organ gave him the perfect opportunity to improve his playing and become an excellent organist. His duties at Arnstadt were not onerous. Three days a week he had to play for church services and teach his students; the rest of the time he could do as liked musically. The necrology records: *Here the first results of his hard work in the art of playing the organ and composing became visible, which he learned by listening to the works of the famous composers of his time and by thinking on his own*. Bach stayed at Arnstadt for four years, until he was 22. Thus, he entered the tradition of Bachs working as civic musicians and organists for almost two centuries in this town. During his years at Arnstadt, Bach composed his first important organ works.

What standard had the art of organ-playing reached in Bach's time? Organ building had achieved a richness and beauty of tone that have arguably never been beaten since. This was particularly due to the organ- and piano-building family of the Silbermanns. Andreas Silbermann, who was born on May 19, 1678 at Kleinbobritzsch near Freiberg in the Saxon Ore Mountains, and who died on March 16, 1734 in Strasbourg, was seven years older than Bach. He died 16 years before Bach. His

11. By building this organ in Freiberg Cathedral, Gottfried Silbermann passed the examination for his master craftsman's certificate in 1714.

12

13

14

12. St. Michael's, Ohrdruf. Oil painting.

13. Lüneberg. Engraving by Conrad Buno.

14. St. Michael's, Lüneburg.

younger brother, Gottfried, was born on January 14, 1683, two years before Bach, and he died on August 4, 1753 in Dresden, three years after Bach. He was the most famous member of the Silbermann family. The life work of the two great organ-builders coincided with Johann Sebastian Bach's career. The two Silbermann brothers built more than 70 big organs. Their craftsmanship in building instruments had a decisive influence on the techniques and richness of tone of organ-building at the time. We do not know how often Bach met Andreas and Gottfried Silbermann, but we do know that four years before Bach died, he and Gottfried Silbermann stayed at Naumburg from September 24-28, 1746 to examine the new organ in the Wenzelskirche constructed by another organ-builder. Naumburg's town council had decided to have *this new work examined and judged by two well-known and technically and musically talented experts.* Thus, Bach and Gottfried Silbermann were invited to *have a close look at the organ, to play it, to examine it, to test it, to list the faults they found and to give expert advice about the organ.* The two men stayed at the 'Green Shield' inn, enjoying free board and lodging. Each of them received a fee of eight ducats after handing in their report at the council chamber in Naumburg.

Andreas Silbermann's eldest son, Johann Andreas, who was born on June 26, 1712 in Strasbourg and who died on February 11, 1783 in Strasbourg, worked in the tradition of his father and uncle. Andreas, Gottfried and Johann Andreas Silbermann built 116 organs within 100 years. Some of these instruments are extant and can still be played. They give aural proof of the technical perfection and rich tone of the organs of Bach's time.

However, we would not do justice to 18th-century organ-building if we confined our comments to Silbermann's organs. There were several other prominent organ builders and all of them influenced the building of instruments in various ways. Bach himself learned the techniques and tones of the organ at an early age. Even as a young man he was known as an organ examiner. The first of his reports that we still have today dates from 1708. In this report about repairing the organ at St. Blasius's in the Thuringian city of Mühlhausen, he advised them 'to repair the organ' entirely. Apart from this report, seven others survive from the period 1711-1746, that is, from Bach's 26th to 61st year. These reports prove that Bach was a technical expert who was asked for advice and criticism by owners of organs, and who was rightly feared and respected by organ-builders. But Bach never considered the technical perfection of an organ to be an end in itself. This became particularly obvious at the end of the extensive report he wrote in May 1716 together with the Cantor of St. Thomas's, Johann Kuhnau, about the organ of the Liebfrauenkirche, Halle:

Furthermore, we hope this organ will always be played to the glory of Almighty God and to the special joy of the honourable patrons and the entire town in peace and for holy encouragement and worship and that it will be played for many years to come. Halle, on the day of the holy Philipp Jacob, 1716.

Great masters create appropriate instruments, and the appropriate instruments find great masters. This is certainly true of the art of organ-playing and organ-building in the 17th and 18th centuries. When 18-year-old Johann Sebastian Bach was first appointed organist at Arnstadt, a number of great musicians had demonstrated their skill at the queen of instruments. All of them were also composers. An organ repertoire as it is known today did not yet exist. From Italy, the fame of Girolamo Frescobaldi, the organist of St. Peter's, Rome, crossed the Alps. From the French court at Versailles, admirable things were told about the art of Louis Marchand. It is said that he later fled a competition with Bach in Dresden, but historians are not sure if this story is true. Carl Philipp Emanuel reported it as second-hand information in his necrology, and it has been celebrated in many German Bach books as an organ victory over the French. But perhaps this is just one of many legends about Bach.

Bach must have impressed his contemporaries very soon with his improvising talents at the organ. According to Carl Philipp Emanuel, the extant compositions of his father's scarcely do justice to Johann Sebastian Bach's unique improvisations. Of course we must assume that the surviving compositions only form a small portion of

15. The organ of St. John's, Lüneburg.

16. Hamburg in Bach's time. Oil painting.

what Johann Sebastian Bach created for the organ in the course of his life. The organists who influenced Bach were not only organists, but also great composers and great improvisers; and the same is true of Bach.

European organ playing had reached the peak of its development in central and northern Germany. Among the famous masters whose compositional techniques and virtuosity had inspired Bach, three were particularly prominent. Like all the masters on the organ of that time, they focused their creative power on the choral prelude, serving the religious purpose of the performance of their art in worship.

Under Italian influence, sacred and secular elements had increasingly been mixed in the choral prelude. It was brought back to the strict fugal form by Johann Pachelbel (1653-1706). For him, the choral prelude was above all a choral fugue. Pachelbel had been

apprenticed to the organist of St. Stephen's, Vienna, as a boy. Later he went to Eisenach and to Erfurt, where he worked for 12 years, after which he moved to Stuttgart and Gotha. At the end of his life, he worked in his father's hometown of Nuremberg, as organist of St. Sebald's. When the young Bach started his career as an organist, Pachelbel's influence in central Germany far exceeded that of any other master. Pachelbel's organ compositions may have a certain rigidity, even monotony, to the ears of today's listeners – at least partly because of the programmatic tendencies of his art. He wanted to restore to organ music the strictness and dignity that he feared could get lost in the exuberant secular melodies of the Italians, particularly Frescobaldi. The difference in character which still exists between the Catholics enjoying the pleasures of life in southern Europe and the strict spirit of evangelical

32

17. Johann Adam Reincken (1623-1722). Oil painting, ascribed to Godfrey Kneller.

Lutheran Christians in central and northern Germany became apparent. Due to Johann Pachelbel and others, the art of organ playing kept its sacred strictness in Germany until Bach's time and later.

As early as his time as a pupil at the grammar school at Lüneburg, Bach listened repeatedly to another famous organ master working at the turn of the 18th century: Georg Böhm (1661-1733). Böhm was appointed organist at St. John's, Lüneburg, in 1698 and worked there until he died. Unlike Pachelbel, he dissolved his choral melodies into opulent coloraturas and elaborate variations. The dignity, sometimes even rigidity and coolness, of Pachelbel's organ compositions are foreign to his nature. In Georg Böhm's chorales, we find the basso ostinato – the continuous repetition of a characteristic motif at the pedal that Bach later often used in his choral preludes.

A third great German organ master influ-

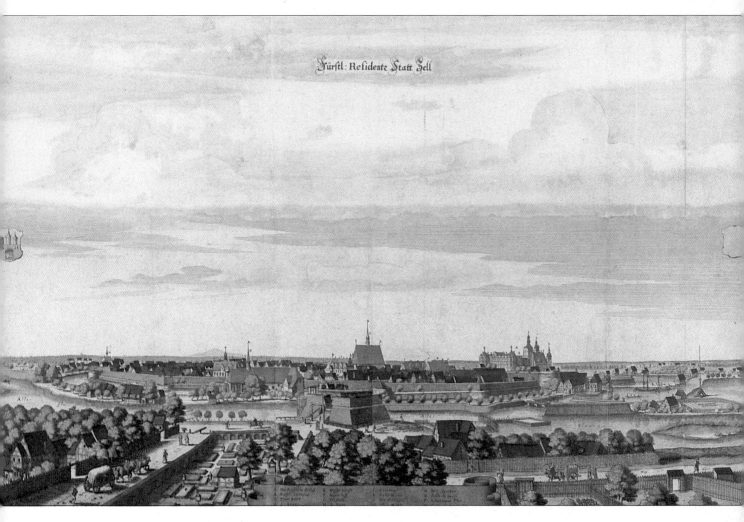

18. The royal seat of Celle. Coloured engraving by Conrad Buno

enced young Bach even more strongly: Dietrich Buxtehude (1637-1707). Since 1668, he had worked as organist at St. Mary's, Lübeck. Bach travelled to Lübeck in November 1705, and probably listened to Buxtehude's famous vespers '*Castrum Doloris*,' the mourning music on the occasion of the death of Emperor Leopold I, and '*Templum Honoris*,' the music honouring his successor Emperor Joseph I, on December 2-3, 1705. The style of the master in Lübeck fell between that of Johann Pachelbel's and that of Georg Böhm. His inspired choral preludes ranged between simple melodies and the most artistic combinations of motifs. Albert Schweitzer - himself a prominent organist - wrote in his Bach biography that Buxtehude should be considered *the real creator of the German organ toccata*. Buxtehude's inventiveness and creative power surpassed the art of the other two masters. He dissolved the melody into brilliant variations without losing them as the centre of his powerful choral preludes.

Albert Schweitzer writes:
These are the forms of choral prelude created by the masters at the end of the 17th century. Formally, they entirely fulfilled their task, since they clearly worked out all possible types of the art. There are three types: One can perform the entire prelude using the motifs of the melodies without touching the latter, but using it as cantus firmus. *That is the way Pachelbel mostly used a motif. Or the melody is dissolved into arabesques so that it*

34

19. Johann Ernst, Duke of Saxe-Weimar (1664-1707). Engraving.

20. Arnstadt

entwines itself around a simple harmony like a blooming creeper. That is the colourful way of Böhm. Or the melody is put at the centre of a free fantasia, as in Buxtehude's choral fantasias. Any other conceivable form of choral prelude is only a mixture of these three basic types that one gets by slightly colouring and decorating the cantus firmus in Pachelbel's choral fugue, or by introducing motifs of the melody into the harmonies con-taining Böhm's choral arabesque, or by having the themes of Buxtehude's fantasia emerge more or less freely from the choral melody. These basic types and mixtures exist-ed when Bach started his career. He did not create any new forms. Neither did Brahms or Reger, modern as they were, because it was impossible. The only difference between Bach and his predecessors was that he transcended the form, but they did not.

Bach summarizes all the traditional forms, refines them and fills them with motifs and life. Form as an end in itself was impossible for Bach. In the synthesis of form and content, his musical genius was fulfilled.

In November 1705, the 20-year-old Johann Sebastian Bach was granted leave of absence from his duties as organist at Arnstadt because he wanted to listen to Buxtehude at Lübeck. Presumably Buxtehude also taught young Johann Sebastian. In any case, Bach did not return to Arnstadt until February 1706 – two months late. He had to answer to the church council for this delay. The records preserved give an insight into the discussions between the angry representatives of the church and the rebellious young organist who did not want to apologize for his behaviour. Thus, the minute dated February 21, 1706 says: *The organist of the Neue Kirche, Bach, is interviewed and asked where he had been for this long time, and who had granted him leave of absence?* Bach's answer: He had been to Lübeck where he had learnt a lot about his craftsmanship, but before his trip, he had asked the superintendent for leave. Whereupon the superintendent said: *Bach had only asked for four weeks off, but took four times four weeks.* Then Bach declared that he hoped *the person who had been appointed to play the organ during his absence had done so without giving cause for any complaints.* This answer seems to have exhausted the patience of the church council; for they accused Bach of *having introduced many foreign variations into the chorales, of having mixed many strange notes into them so that the congregation had been confused.* Bach was given detailed instructions as to how he had to play the organ in the future. Finally, the church council added that they were not happy with the way he instructed his pupils in music. Bach on the other hand blamed the circumstances.

A pupil was called and interviewed *about the disorders . . . between the pupils and the organist.* The pupil explained in detail: *Until then, the organist Bach had played a bit too long. But after the superintendent had spoken to him about this fact, he had gone to the other extreme and had played very briefly.* Obviously Bach succeeded in proving that he was not to blame for the disagreements, since the minute ends with the decision that the pupil who had been interviewed had to spend two hours in the cell on four consecutive days.

Following this glimpse of everyday life at Arnstadt in 1706, the tensions remained. Nine months later, in November 1706, Bach again had to answer to the church council for having neglected his duties. Again Bach was accused by the council of having neglected the musical instruction of the pupils. Bach promised to hand in a written statement about this accusation, but according to the records, he never wrote this statement. Besides, he was accused of having allowed an unknown young woman to come to the church gallery to make music. Such things were strictly forbidden for an organist of 1707. That this 'unknown young woman' was Bach's cousin and later wife, Maria Barbara, as some authors assume, cannot be proved.

The church council even had to deal with the obstinate young organist six months before Bach's delayed return from Lübeck, regarding Bach's fight with a pupil. According to Bach, he had returned home from Arnstadt Castle late at night and met a group of six pupils in front of the town hall. One of the pupils, by the name of Geyersbach, attacked him with a club, because allegedly Bach had offended him. To defend himself, Bach had drawn his rapier. Then Geyersbach hit his arm. According to the minute, other pupils hurried to separate the two brawlers. Bach reported this incident to the police the next day. According to the records, the council met four times to listen to the charges and counter-charges and interview witnesses. Bach's cousin, Barbara Katharina, the elder sister of Bach's wife-to-be Maria Barbara, who had accompanied Bach that night, witnessed the truth of her cousin's words. The pupil Geyersbach was alleged to have beaten Bach in the face, whereupon the latter had drawn his rapier, though without touching the pupil with the weapon. Because of the contradictory reports of the witnesses which can be read throughout the minutes we cannot reconstruct why this fight started and what really happened. Neither do the records tell what verdict was finally pronounced, and if Geyersbach was punished as Bach demanded.

Reading what happened at Arnstadt, the observer living three centuries later recognizes two things. Even in his youth, Bach must have been a self-opinionated, self-assured man who had a mind of his own. And from the beginning, he had difficulties instructing pupils. His pedagogic skills were in contrast to his musical genius. This is true both of the young Bach at Arnstadt and of the later choirmaster and teacher at St. Thomas's, Leipzig.

21. The Holstentor and St. Mary's, Lübeck.

22. Minutes of the church council of Arnstadt concerning J.S. Bach.

Johann Sebastian Bach

Mühlhausen

In the spring of 1707, an opportunity arose for Bach to flee the strained atmosphere at Arnstadt which he had at least partly caused himself. The organist at St. Blasius's, in the Thuringian free town of Mühlhausen, had died. Bach was invited to give a trial performance on Easter Sunday. The inhabitants of Mühlhausen were so impressed by the skilful organ playing of the 22-year-old Johann Sebastian Bach that the town clerk (who was related to the Bach family by marriage) was asked to negotiate with Bach. Three weeks later, in the middle of June 1707, Bach was appointed organist at St. Blasius's. His salary consisted of 85 gulden a year and a payment in kind of three quarters of corn, two fathoms of wood and six bundles of brushwood – an average income at the time. Bach's predecessor, Johann Georg Ahle, had been paid a lower salary by the town council, although he had been organist for 30 years. Neither did Bach's successor at Mühlhausen receive the salary Bach had been paid. Both Bach's business sense and the respect with which the authorities regarded him became obvious at Mühlhausen. Besides, we can assume that the town clerk who was related to him helped ensure that the young Bach was well paid. The authorities always respected Bach's extraordinary musical abilities, of course without knowing that his importance would extend beyond their time. The musical culture of that time can only be envied by today's musicians. While today an artist needs publicity in order to be noticed, not to mention respected, in Bach's time it was enough to master

one's art better than others to gain respect.

At Mühlhausen the evangelical Lutheran Bach was treading on historic ground. Thomas Müntzer, the spiritual leader of the Anabaptists, had lived in this town. From the free town on the river Unstrut he had spread his message of a revolutionary Christianity over the German states and fanned the flame of the peasants' revolts into war. Müntzer's theological controversies with Luther, whom he accused of making a pact with the ruling leaders, created a revolutionary tradition in Mühlhausen which even made Karl Marx visit this town centuries later. The Mühlhausen where Bach became organist in the summer of 1707 was filled with spiritual unrest. The musical tradition which had been developed by Bach's predecessors in the town in the 16th and 17th centuries was overshadowed by the fierce discussions between orthodox Lutherans and Pietists which took place in many of its Protestant churches. While for orthodox Lutherans music was very important in church, the young Pietist movement tried to reduce the role of church music. Bach's superior at the church of St. Blasius, superintendent Johann Adolph Frohne, was a supporter of this Pietist movement, opposing sacred music. On the other hand, the pastor of neighbouring St. Mary's church, Georg Christian Eilmar, supported the orthodox view. Eilmar had worked on the text of Bach's first cantata. Later he became godfather to Bach's first child. Clearly Bach stood between the theological fronts. He did so very well, strengthened by the fact that the two compe-

24. Bach's organ at Arnstadt.

theological fronts. He did so very well, strengthened by the fact that the two competing pastors liked him personally.

The first major event in Bach's life during his two years at Mühlhausen was his wedding. His fiancée was his second cousin Maria Barbara Bach, born on October 20, 1684. The wedding ceremony took place in the village church of Dornheim, near Arnstadt. In the marriage register of this church we read:

On October 17, 1707, Mr Johann Sebastian Bach, an unmarried man and organist at St. Blasius's, Mühlhausen, legitimate son of the late Mr Ambrosius Bach, a respected town organist and musician at Eisenach, married spinster Maria Barbara Bach, the youngest daughter of the late Mr Johann Michael Bach, respected organist at Gehren, here in our church, after putting up the banns at Arnstadt.

The second important event took place a few months later, when Bach composed his first extant cantata, 'Gott ist mein König' (God is my king; BWV 71). Its other name, 'Mühlhauser Ratswechselkantate' (cantata for the change of council at Mühlhausen) refers to the occasion for which the cantata was composed. Conducted by Bach, it was performed on February 4, 1708 at St. Mary's on the occasion of the festival service marking the beginning of the term of office of the new councillors of Mühlhausen. The text was taken from the Old Testament. The verses praising God's omnipotence, the new town council and Emperor Joseph I were written by pastor Eilmar and Bach together. With its four instrumental parts, its alternation between solo and choral singing and its magnificent arias between the strict choral fugues, this Mühlhausen composition is one of Bach's early masterpieces, leading the way to the great cantatas of his creative periods at Weimar and Leipzig. 'Gott ist mein König' is the only surviving cantata by Bach for which

voice parts were printed during his lifetime, though the music was printed to honour the occasion and not the young composer. But at the same time, the councillors and inhabitants of Mühlhausen recorded their acceptance of Bach's early work.

Bach's other compositions at Mühlhausen continued the clavier and organ works of his years at Arnstadt. But composing was only part of Bach's musical work. The technical and organisational requirements for a *regulated sacred music to God's honour* were as important to him as was writing down notes. He wanted to improve sacred music at Mühlhausen, and was not content with the organ at St. Blasius's. Encouraged by the success of his cantata, he proposed to repair the organ and wrote an exact specification for the necessary repair works. The councillors eventually agreed to his plan and instructed the organ builder Johann Friedrich Wender from Mühlhausen to carry out the work. Bach had played Wender's organ at Arnstadt for four years. Although Bach left Mühlhausen before the organ was repaired, the councillors asked him to supervise the repair of the organ from nearby Weimar. This perhaps indicates that the inhabitants of Mühlhausen did not want to let Bach go at all. This is recorded in the minutes of the council's meeting on June 26, 1708: *Because it is impossible to keep him, we have no alternative but to accept his resignation.*

There were two decisive reasons why Bach left Mühlhausen so soon, although he was met there with a respect which was unusual for his youth. By moving to the court at Weimar, he could enormously improve his personal income, whereas the inadequate payment for church music at Mühlhausen hardly gave him any opportunity to improve his situation. A few months before Bach took up his job at Mühlhausen, a fire had destroyed a quarter of the town's living area,

25. Mühlhausen in the 17th century. Coloured engraving.

including some of the most beautiful and richest buildings within the parish of St. Blasius's. The inhabitants were concerned with other things than musical performances. Bach's complaint about his high rent at Mühlhausen was further proof of the hard times in town. The theological argument between orthodox and Pietist Christians is mentioned in Bach's letter of resignation when he speaks of *adversity*. This dispute affected his work. The *ultimate aim of church music without offending others* seems to refer to Bach's wish to perform cantatas, which regularly met with superintendent Frohne's objections. On June 26, 1708, Bach handed in the following letter of resignation:

Your Magnificence, Honoured and Noble Sirs, Honoured and Learned Sirs, Honoured and Wise Sirs, Most Gracious Patrons and Gentlemen!,

I will always be obliged and thankful to the Honourable and Respected Councillors for appointing my modest self to the vacant post of organist at St. Blasius's and for paying me an appropriate salary. I would have liked to work towards the ultimate aim of church music – a well-regulated church music to God's honour – according to their will and besides would have liked to assist the development of church music played in almost all of the villages and the harmony which is often better there than it is here and, therefore, I bought a good stock of selected pieces of church music. In addition, I dutifully handed in a report which started the project of repairing the defects in the organ, and I should gladly have discharged every other duty of my office – yet it has not been possible to accomplish all this without hindrance, and there are, at present, hardly any signs

26. Johann Adolph Frohne (1652-1713).
Oil painting.

27. Georg Christian Eilmar (1665-1715).
Oil painting.

that in the future such a change may take place. Besides, I must humbly say that I am living in very poor conditions due to the high rent and other necessary things I have to pay.

God has unexpectedly opened another opportunity to me where I can improve my living conditions and can continue pursuing my aim with regard to sacred music without causing anyone further trouble. I am offered the position of court Kapellmeister and chamber musician at the court of His Majesty, the Prince of Saxe-Weimar. I hereby inform my honourable patrons of this offer with all due respect. At the same time I ask you to do me the favour of releasing me from my services at church. If I am able to contribute anything to the church at Mühlhausen, I will do so not with words but with deeds.

Honourable and Respected Patrons,
Your obedient servant,
Joh. Seb. Bach
Mühlhausen, 25 June, 1708.

Bach's letter of resignation did not deny that he was discontented and aspired to better living conditions, but at the same time he diplomatically sustained the good relationship he had with the people at Mühlhausen even after leaving the town. Thus, at the councillors' special request, he composed a cantata to celebrate the inauguration of the new councillors in the following year, as we read in the council records dated February 7, 1709. In the files, an entry about the costs of printing the cantata can be found, but sadly the cantata itself has not been preserved. Bach remained on friendly terms with pastor Eilmar and his family. It can be assumed that he played the organ repaired by Wender when it was officially inaugurated, and probably travelled from Weimar to Mühlhausen on many other occasions. Even 26 years later he

28. Mühlhausen, with St. Mary's.

wrote a report about the organ, and found a
job for his son Johann Gottfried Bernhard as
organist at St. Mary's by referring to *their
long-lasting favour*.

Weimar

Bach now went to Weimar. He was familiar with the musical situation at the royal capital, due to his brief employment as a violinist in the chamber orchestra of the co-regnant Duke Johann Ernst, his employer's younger brother. From Mühlhausen, he had come into contact with Weimar and was *offered the position of court Kapellmeister and chamber musician at the court of His Majesty, the Prince of Saxe-Weimar*, as he wrote in his letter of resignation to the church council at Mühlhausen. This procedure was characteristic of Bach's prudence. He never mentioned leaving his position to his employers until he was certain of improving his situation by the planned change. He did this even as a young man who did not yet have to provide for a big family.

Bach's first employer at Weimar, Duke Johann Ernst, had died in 1707. But through his two sons, Prince Ernst August and his half-brother Prince Johann Ernst, Bach had a personal relationship with the court at Weimar. He was a frequent guest at the Red Castle where the two princes lived. They were talented musicians, and Bach became their teacher. Prince Ernst August succeeded his father as co-regent in 1709, whilst his younger brother, Johann Ernst, became well-known as a composer of instrumental music in the Italian style. Bach used some of Johann Ernst's concertos as models for his own organ and clavier transcriptions, preserving for them a place in the history of music.

As a chamber musician and court organist, Bach was at the service of Duke Wilhelm Ernst who resided at the castle of Wilhelmsburg. The duke, who was 46 when Bach assumed his post, was regarded as one of the most artistic princes of his time. His court orchestra consisted of some 20 musicians. Most of them worked as hunters, cooks and lackeys besides playing music, as was usual at the time. Whether Bach sometimes wore the uniform of a retainer is unknown. When he started work at Weimar, his salary was twice the salary he had received at Mühlhausen, and within the first five years it rose to three times the sum. When he was promoted to the post of concertmaster at the age of 29, in 1714, this meant another rise in salary. The duke seems to have appreciated Bach's abilities highly.

Wilhelm Ernst was a devout, highly moral man whose simple way of living was in contrast to the dissipated life of many princes of his time. However, this puritanical attitude did not prevent him from promoting art and science whenever he could. For him, any artistic performance had its ultimate meaning in religion. In this regard, his spiritual viewpoint coincided with Bach's. The duke gathered around him a number of scholars and connoisseurs, among them Salomon Franck. The latter was consistorial secretary, librarian and curator of the coin collection and also court poet at Weimar. In him, Bach found an able librettist for the texts of his cantatas. At the civic church in Weimar, Bach's cousin, Johann Gottfried Walther, who was the same age as Bach, worked as organist. Later he became the editor of the first German musical

29. Church and choirmaster's house, Gehren. Oil painting by Voigt.
Bach came here frequently to visit his parents-in-law while he was at Weimar.

30. Street in front of the town hall, Mühlhausen, where Bach remained a welcome visitor.

31. Dornheim church, where Bach married in 1707. His family grew rapidly during his years at Weimar.

encyclopaedia, which remains one of the most important reference books on music and musicians of that time. Walther, a capable composer himself, had a great and reciprocal influence upon Bach. Johann Matthias Gesner, later rector of St Thomas's school in Leipzig, and a man who helped Bach when he was in need, came to Weimar in 1715 as deputy head of the grammar school. His personality had a positive influence on the royal capital. Thus, young Bach found a scholarly, cosmopolitan circle of people at Weimar who supported his spiritual, musical and human progress. The nine years Bach stayed at Weimar, from the age of 23 to 32, proved decisive for his spiritual and musical development.

The royal capital of Saxe-Weimar gave a modest, almost impoverished, impression at the beginning of the 18th century. In 1785, the population of the entire dukedom was only 106,398 people, as recorded in a census dating from that year. Only 6000 of these people lived at Weimar. Thus we have to assume that, at the beginning of the 18th century, not more than 4000 people lived at the royal capital of Weimar and in the little surrounding towns. Medieval fortifications and a wall with four gates encircled about 500 houses, most of which were low buildings with roofs of thatch or shingles. Standing out from these houses were a few town houses, the market square and town hall built in the Renaissance style, and the church steeples. The centre of religious and cultural life was the castle. At Bach's time, nobody had any idea that only a century later this picturesque little town in the valley of the river Ilme would become the centre of German literary life.

As a chamber musician, Bach was a member of the court orchestra. Besides the organ, he also played the violin, viola and harpsichord. The duties of the court orchestra included performances of sacred music on Sundays, musical entertainment at social events, chamber music, serenades and other performances of religious and secular music. Bach soon also served as a composer and arranger in order to relieve the load of court Kapellmeister, Johann Samuel Drese. The latter was well advanced in years and was often substituted for by his son Johann Wilhelm, a mediocre musician. This was to be one of the reasons for Bach's later conflict with the duke.

Freed from the interference of superiors, Bach's genius at the organ could develop itself to the full in the castle chapel of Weimar. In Bach's early organ compositions, we do not find the strict style that distinguishes his later works, but rather a variety of forms and influences that can be traced back to great models. Like many other young artists, Bach took existing forms and transformed them. In his preludes and fugues he proved himself an apt student of Frescobaldi and Buxtehude – they are dramatic, often unbalanced compositions. His organ works gained clarity in musical form as he encountered the works of Arcangelo Corelli and Antonio Vivaldi. At Weimar, Bach rid himself of the constraints of the great masters of his time. At last he found his own way. His themes became simpler and clearer; the fugues became stricter, sometimes even unadorned. Bach's impulsive spirit finally accepted the laws of form. Taming his virtuosity and musical imagination with the self-discipline of strict forms created the elemental power which can be heard in Bach's mature organ compositions.

Bach's son Carl Philipp Emanuel, born at Weimar in 1714, was too young to speak from his own experience of the organ works his father created in the royal capital. But his words are based on the reports of witnesses: *The pleasure the honourable lords derived from his playing encouraged him to try any-*

Prod. 9. 25. Jun. 1708.

32. Bach's letter of resignation dated June 25, 1708 to the council of the free town of Mühlhausen.

thing possible in the art of organ playing. He composed most of his organ works at Weimar. From Weimar, Bach's reputation as an organ virtuoso spread to the other German states. Students came and learned under him. He was often asked for his opinion of organs. Carl Philipp Emanuel reported:

Never before had anybody examined organs so strictly and at the same time so honestly. He was to a very high degree familiar with the entire art of organ-building. When an organ-builder had done a good job, but not been paid enough, Bach made the patrons pay him more. Nobody could pull out the organ stops as he did. Organists often became frightened when he wanted to play their organs and pulled out the stops, since they believed it could never sound as good as he wanted it to sound, but they were astonished at what these instruments could do. . . When examining an organ, he first of all said: I must know if this organ has good lungs. In order to find out, he pulled out everything that gave a sound and played with as many voices as possible. When he did so, organ builders often turned pale with fear. He laid great stress on tuning his instruments and on tuning the instruments of the entire orchestra. Nobody could tune or quill his instruments to his satisfaction. He did everything himself.

(Quilling is cutting the quill for the harpsichord.)

In the necrology, Carl Philipp Emanuel reports:

All his fingers were perfectly trained. All of them were able to do a refined and meticulous job. He had discovered a comfortable fingering so that it was not hard for him to perform even the most difficult pieces fluently and without problems. Before him, the most famous clavier players in Germany and other countries rarely used their thumbs. But he knew how to use his thumbs in a fascinating way. With his two feet, he could perform movements on the pedals which would be hard for many a skilful clavier player to do using five fingers.

Reading these words by his son, it is not hard to imagine what a masterly improviser Bach must have been at the organ.

On March 2, 1714, he was appointed concertmaster *ranking after vice-Kapellmeister Drese.* According to the duke's instructions, he now had to *perform one new cantata every month. The musicians of the orchestra had to come to the rehearsals, if so required by Bach.* Bach himself had requested this appointment. It meant that from 1714 on he had to perform twelve church cantatas a year. This brought him nearer to the *ultimate aim of church music.* From the last four years Bach spent at Weimar, some three dozen cantatas are extant; unfortunately, many of the others seem to be lost forever.

We live in a profane age. Many contemporaries no longer see singing and music-making as an indispensable part of worship. When the all-embracing reality of faith is lost, the immediate experience of religious art is broken. It is replaced by an aesthetic or historical way of looking at things. This is the only way to explain why nowadays the Bach renaissance focuses its interest and interpretation on his secular works, concertos, piano pieces and chamber music, although the sacred cantatas (some 200 of which have been preserved) form the dominant part of his extant works, even numerically. It is reckoned that Bach composed some 300 church cantatas during his lifetime. About a third of his sacred vocal works have been lost. We do not know how many secular cantatas have been lost, too – some 40 have been preserved. Only quite recently has the number of extant cantatas been made comprehensible for non-experts. In 1971, Alfred Dürr published his exhaustive book '*Die Kantaten von Johann*

33. The castle at Weimar, called 'Wilhelmsburg.' Water-colour.

34. Johann Sebastian Bach as concertmaster at Weimar. Oil painting, probably by Johann Ernst Rentsch the Elder, around 1715. The authenticity of this picture is controversial.

35. The castle chapel at Weimar. Gouache by Christian Richter c. 1660.

Sebastian Bach', the first systematic presentation of Bach's cantatas. With scientific precision, it summarizes all the research to date.

A milestone on the way to rediscovering Bach's cantatas was the first issue by Hänssler CLASSIC of all church cantatas on 100 long-playing records in 1985. Now they are included in the edition of Bach's complete works on 172 CDs by Hänssler CLASSIC. The excellent interpretation of the cantatas in this set by Helmuth Rilling and his Bach orchestra superseded the styles in previous recordings. Dürr's book and the complete recording by Rilling finally offered the long-desired overview of Bach's cantatas to those perform-

ing Bach's works and to all Bach lovers.

Although Bach composed the majority of his cantatas in Leipzig some years later, a survey of all the cantatas makes clear the importance of Bach's turning to composing cantatas in his last years at Weimar. In the introduction to his book, about the history of cantatas before Bach, Alfred Dürr writes:

In the 17th and at the beginning of the 18th century, the cantata was prominent among the genres of music. The cantata was closely related to the opera and the oratorio, and first came into being as a lyrical counterpart to these dramatic and epic genres in Italy. However, it reached neighbouring

55

countries in the course of the 17th century and reached a unique climax in Protestant Germany as the church cantata. This climax, however, is inseparable from the name of Johann Sebastian Bach.

Luther's conviction that God's word can only blossom in the hearts and spirits of people when it is proclaimed in a lively way was the starting-point for Pietist church cantatas. The gospel, its interpretation in preaching and its musical interpretation in the various cantatas, formed the centre of worship. In the early form of church cantata, verses from the Bible and spiritual songs were the only source of libretti. The composers set these texts to music, alternating freely between arias and choral movements. Only a few free stanzas were added to the texts of the Bible or hymns. From Heinrich Schütz, whose vocal works were an early highlight of church cantatas two generations after Luther, to Dietrich Buxtehude, this text form which determines the musical flow had not been changed.

In his early years, Bach composed his first cantatas in the same style, alternating between instrumental introductory and linking movements, arias and chorales. But as the Italian madrigal progressed and finally gained acceptance in Germany at the beginning of the 18th century, the libretti became more important. Free numbers of stanzas, blind rhymes, different line lengths, even changes of metre granted a poetic liberty to the madrigal poet which opened up entirely new possibilities for the symbiosis of word and music. In sacred poetry, the original secular madrigal reached a final amazing peak. *'Madrigalian Joy of the Soul about the Suffering of Our Redeemer'* is the title of a volume of poems published by Salomon Franck in 1697. The poet Erdmann Neumeister, who was court chaplain at nearby Weissenfels until 1715, was the first librettist who consistently applied the madri-

gal form to the church cantata. In 1700, he published the first volume of his cantata libretti. Nine others were to follow. In 1704, the first volume was published in book form, with the title *'Spiritual Cantatas instead of Church Music'*. In his preface, Neumeister proclaimed: *In a word, a cantata is not much different from a section of an opera, composed of recitative style and arias.*

Bach composed some 20 cantatas with libretti by Salomon Franck at Weimar. Twice he used libretti by Erdmann Neumeister and twice spiritual poems by Georg Christian Lehms, who lived as a court poet and librarian at Darmstadt. Even at Leipzig, Bach used the cantata texts of these librettists. First, he composed three cantatas without recitatives to Franck's libretti. The old form of cantata – chorus, arias, final chorale – was not changed. Even later, he sometimes used this form. But then he changed to the form of the recitative and the instrumentally-accompanied aria, using the texts by Neumeister. The other cantata texts by Salomon Franck were set in this form, too. Bach's inexhaustible inventiveness became particularly visible in the way he arranged the chorus. The richness of his music, and the variety of his forms, freed him from the rigid schemes to which many composers of the 18th century fell victim. Bach's genius did not prove itself by his detaching himself from the forms of his time, but by his mastering them better than his contemporaries and filling them with music of greater substance. The wonderful liveliness of Bach's cantatas, which reached maturity during his time at Weimar, grew out of a conjunction of the musical and the dramatic, a lyrical-mystical commitment to faith and an unprecedented variety of forms where words and music united into something greater. Bach had available to him not only the poetic texts of the cantatas just mentioned, but also a number of other texts.

36. Wilhelm Ernst, Duke of Saxe-Weimar (1662-1728). Oil painting.

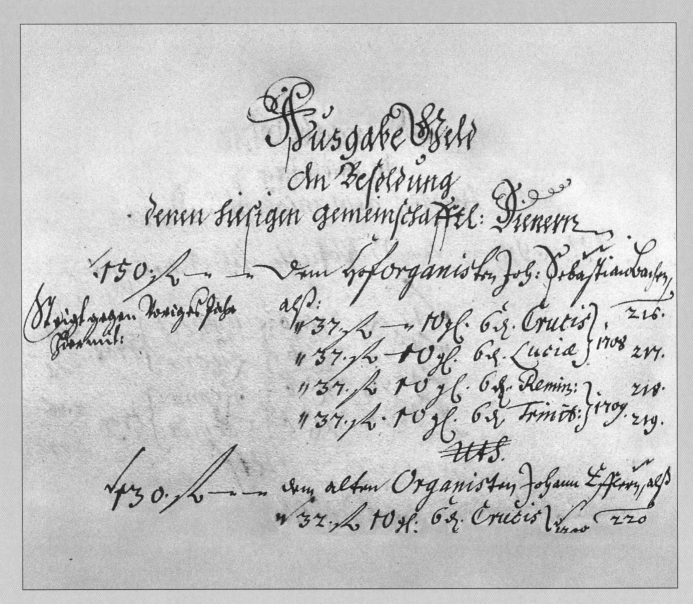

37. Accounts of the payments to Bach at Weimar, 1708-1709.

Bach's legacy included not only the Bible, but also the eight volumes of the *'Leipzig Songbook'*, dating from 1697. One can assume that this book was in his possession as early as his time at Weimar. It contains more than 5,000 hymns, from the Middle Ages to the sacred poems by Paul Gerhardt. When Bach left Weimar, the conditions were set for his cantatas, both with regard to their contents and their form. As Alfred Dürr says in summarizing his study of Bach's Weimar cantatas:

The new things he created at Cöthen and Leipzig were first of all an expansion of existing forms, a variation on the opportunities he was offered. . . But there was no fundamental change like the one Bach underwent at Weimar, from the old to the new form of cantatas.

During the nine years he lived at Weimar, radical changes took place in Bach's personal life, too. The young man became the head of a family that increased in size very quickly. His circle of friends and acquaintances grew. He became acquainted with numerous con-

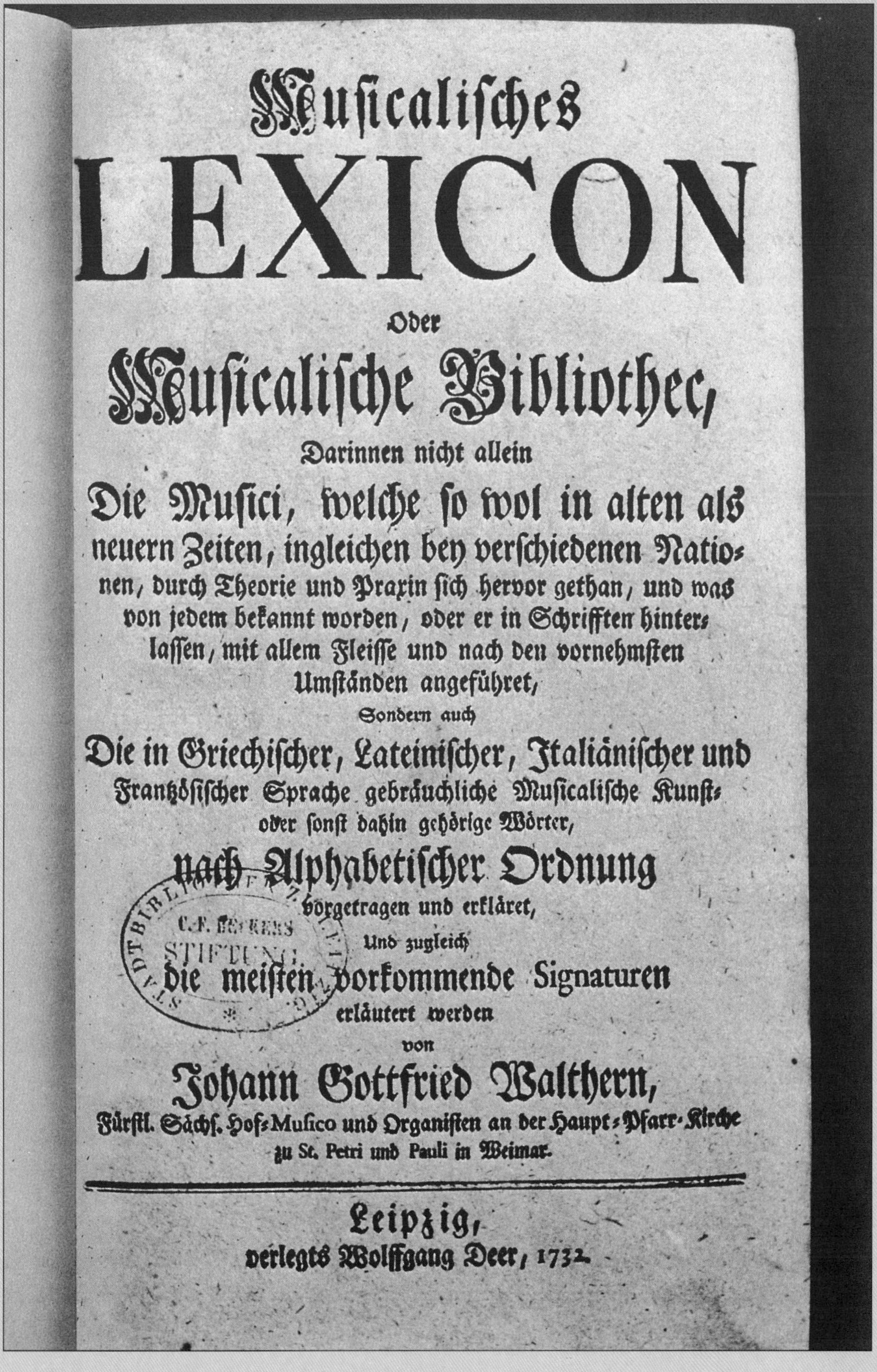

Musicalisches
LEXICON

Oder

Musicalische Bibliothec,

Darinnen nicht allein

Die Musici, welche so wol in alten als
neuern Zeiten, ingleichen bey verschiedenen Natio-
nen, durch Theorie und Praxin sich hervor gethan, und was
von jedem bekannt worden, oder er in Schrifften hinter-
lassen, mit allem Fleisse und nach den vornehmsten
Umständen angeführet,

Sondern auch

Die in Griechischer, Lateinischer, Italiänischer und
Frantzösischer Sprache gebräuchliche Musicalische Kunst-
oder sonst dahin gehörige Wörter,

nach Alphabetischer Ordnung

vorgetragen und erkläret,

Und zugleich

die meisten vorkommende Signaturen
erläutert werden

von

Johann Gottfried Walthern,

Fürstl. Sächs. Hof-Musico und Organisten an der Haupt-Pfarr-Kirche
zu St. Petri und Pauli in Weimar.

Leipzig,

verlegts Wolffgang Deer, 1732.

38. Johann Gottfried Walther's 'Musical Encyclopedia'.

temporary musicians. Contact was made with neighbouring royal courts.

Repeated stays at nearby towns and offers from other towns contributed to making the young organist a musical personality whose name became well-known throughout the German states. Happiness and success – and later bitter personal disappointment – marked this decade at Weimar. In December 1708, Bach's first child, Catharina Dorothea, was born. In November 1710, Wilhelm Friedemann was born, and in February 1713, his wife gave birth to twins who died soon after being born. In March 1714, Carl Philipp Emanuel saw the light of day. Georg Philipp Telemann was one of his three godfathers. In May 1715, Johann Gottfried Bernhard was born – six children in seven years. The accounts in the books preserved in several church archives in central Germany indicate that beside the salary he received at Weimar, Bach had an additional income from assessing organs in these years.

Everyday things finally caused Bach to leave Weimar. Disagreements between the two ducal lines increased to the extent that the reigning Duke Wilhelm Ernst forbade the members of the court orchestra, on threat of a fine, from serving in the wing of the castle where his nephew, Ernst August, lived. The 'common servants' – among them the musicians – had always served the courts of both dukes, as is attested in documents. The order bothered Bach even more since he had a

39. The civic church, Weimar. Engraving.

friendly relationship with the young Duke Ernst August and his wife. This affection had deepened after the early death of the duke's half-brother Johann Ernst. The early death of the 18-year-old prince, whose teaching by Johann Gottfried Walther and by Bach had made him excellent musician, left Bach shattered. He disobeyed Duke Wilhelm Ernst's instructions and thus incurred his displeasure with serious consequences. On December 1, 1716, the aged court Kapellmeister Drese died. The duke first tried to attract as his successor Georg Philipp Telemann, who worked at Frankfurt-am-Main. When Telemann declined his offer, he appointed Drese's son to the post of new court Kapellmeister. Bach, who had long since become the leading light of court music at Weimar, felt ignored, deeply offended and hurt. He immediately restricted his musical activities to the absolutely necessary and stopped composing cantatas. From that time on he sought a way to leave Weimar as soon as possible. Young Duke Ernst August and his wife, Eleonore Wilhelmine, a sister of Prince Leopold of Anhalt-Cöthen, seem to have helped him in finding new opportunities.

On August 5, 1717, Prince Leopold appointed Bach court Kapellmeister and *Director of Our Chamber Music* of Anhalt-Cöthen. From the same month, payments to Bach are recorded in the archives of Cöthen. At this date, Bach was still in the service of the Duke of Weimar. The tone with which he requested his immediate release met with the duke's disapproval, to the extent that he had Bach arrested before letting him go *because of his obstinate behaviour and the way he wanted to force through his dismissal.* This was the official explanation for Bach's arrest *in the judge's chambers* from November 6 until December 2, 1717. By this action, the duke showed the rebellious musician Bach (as well as his ducal relations) who held the power at Weimar. His nephew, Ernst August, his wife and the court at Cöthen seemed unimpressed by this demonstration of absolutist power. They responded in their own way. On November 17, 1718, Prince Leopold, his sister Eleonore Wilhelmine, Duchess of Saxe-Weimar by marriage, their brother, Prince August Ludwig, and the Court Councillor at Cöthen and the wife of the Court Minister at Cöthen stood godparents to Bach's seventh child, a son. He was baptized in the court chapel of Cöthen and given the Christian names Leopold August. This heavily symbolic action showed both the respect for Bach in his new home and the godparents' displeasure at the way the ducal relative at Weimar had dismissed Bach.

40. The castle area, Weimar. Gouache.

Cöthen

At Christmas 1717, Bach took up his new post as court Kapellmeister at Cöthen. He was now director of the chamber music orchestra of a German provincial capital where the arts were appreciated. At Cöthen, people had more freedom; the atmosphere at court was more relaxed than at the strictly orthodox Weimar, which was ruled in an absolutist way. The landscape around Cöthen was more expansive too; on sunny days, the horizon was brighter than in the valley of the river Ilme, some 75 miles (120 kilometres) south-west of Cöthen. The court at Cöthen was Calvinistic rather than Lutheran, as at Weimar. At Cöthen, Bach was not expected to play or compose sacred music. Musical life was focused on secular music, on playing music for fun and joy, on performances at court, and on social entertainment. Thus, Bach composed almost only secular music at Cöthen. An exception was the church cantata, no longer extant, which he composed for Prince Leopold's 24th birthday celebrated on December 10, 1718.

Bach's new employer was almost ten years younger than the court Kapellmeister; he was a young man who had travelled far and was well educated musically. The prince played the violin, viola da gamba and harpsichord, and was a member of the court orchestra consisting of 18 musicians. Prince Leopold recognized Bach's genius. He was proud of his new court Kapellmeister and asked Bach to join him on his travels. Sometimes half a dozen court musicians followed them in royal coaches, accompanying the prince and his director of music. In this way they could continue making music even when they were away from Cöthen. They were excellent musicians – some of them had come from far away – who made court music at Cöthen under Kapellmeister Bach well-known far beyond the borders of the principality.

Prince Leopold and Bach soon became friends, and this personal friendship continued after Bach left Cöthen. Numerous compositions by Bach, even in later years, were dedicated to the prince and his family. The six years Bach spent at Anhalt-Cöthen were the happiest, most carefree years in his life as a musician. The prince paid him the same salary as was paid to the major-domo, the highest office-holder at court. Thus, Bach was free from any material worries, despite his many children. A shadow fell across this happiness when Bach's son, Leopold August, died at the age of only one year.

In the 18th century, infant mortality was high, and Christians accepted it piously. The medical struggle to save human life which nowadays often starts even before a child is born was unknown at the time; however, parents found much comfort in their faith when they had to bury their children. But we must not underestimate the pain our ancestors endured during their frequent walks to the cemetery. This was also true for Johann Sebastian Bach. The heavy load women had to bear can hardly be imagined today. Many of them collapsed under their heavy burden. As did Maria Barbara Bach. Three months before her 36th birthday, she was buried at Cöthen, on July 7, 1720. The cause of her death is not documented. Bach did not hear of her death until several days later, when he returned home from a journey to Karlsbad with the prince.

Bach was 36 years old. Three of the seven children Maria Barbara had borne had died; four of them were alive. The firstborn, Catharina Dorothea, who was born at Christmas 1708, was 12. The eldest son, Wilhelm Friedemann, who was born on November 22, 1710, was ten; his brother Carl Philipp Emanuel, who was born on March 8, 1714, was six. The youngest child, Johann Gottfried Bernhard, born on May 11, 1715, had just celebrated his fifth birthday. One and a half years after Maria Barbara's death, Bach married again: his second wife, Anna Magdalena Wilcke, was the youngest daughter of Johann Caspar Wilcke, the court trumpeter at Weissenfels. Bach had been in touch with the royal capital of Saxony-Weissenfels since the time when he lived at Weimar. In 1713, he had visited this town in the entourage of Duke Wilhelm Ernst and had performed his cantata 'Was mir behagt, ist nur die muntre Jagd' (All I like is hunting; BWV 208) at the birthday party of Duke Christian, a keen huntsman. Salomon Franck had written the text for this cantata. Perhaps Bach came to know the court trumpeter Wilcke and his family during this visit. Duke Christian later bestowed upon Bach the title of 'Court Kapellmeister of Weissenfels'.

The name of Anna Magdalena Wilcke, a trained soprano, is listed at the court of Cöthen among the 'prince's female singers' as early as in 1721, even before she married court Kapellmeister Bach. In this year and in 1722, after she had become Mrs Johann Sebastian Bach, monthly payments to her were recorded. Anna Magdalena was sixteen years younger than Bach. Not only was she a loving wife and a patient stepmother to his four motherless children; but the 21-year-old woman also brought a deep artistic understanding to the marriage to court Kapellmeister Bach. The two years Bach remained at Cöthen after their wedding were clearly influenced by this young woman. She was to play an important part in Bach's future creative work. Many sentimental legends have been told about Anna Magdalena Bach, but before looking at the few facts that are known about her, it is worth mentioning a professional step Bach made – presumably for private reasons.

A few months after the death of his first wife, in November 1720, Bach applied for the vacant post of organist at St. James's church, Hamburg, whose organist had died. Hamburg's reputation as a city of music, and the famous organ of St. James's, a four-manual masterpiece by Arp Schnitger, certainly contributed to Bach's plans to move to Hamburg; as well as the fact that Erdmann Neumeister had been senior pastor at St. James's since 1715. After his wife's death, Bach, who was a very religious man, probably had a desire to return to sacred music. Another reason for this step may have been a wish to leave Cöthen. The surviving documents of St. James' church, however, show that Bach did not seriously pursue his application. Besides Bach, seven other musicians applied for the post. Apparently Bach did not give a trial performance on November 28, 1720, *because Mr Bach had to accompany his prince on a journey on November 23*, as is recorded in the minutes of St. James's. The election of the new organist, planned for December 12, was postponed, because the committee wanted to wait for news from Bach. On December 19, the minutes recorded:

Mr Luttas had tried to postpone the decision until he should receive a letter from Mr

Johann Sebastian Bach, Kapellmeister at Cöthen. The pastor and the patrons of the church had agreed. Meanwhile, Mr Luttas has received a letter. He informed the pastor and the patrons of its contents and later read it to the assembly.

This letter from Bach has not survived. In the minutes, nothing was mentioned about any request by Bach for a new date for a trial performance. The quoted letter can only have been a withdrawal of his application or an attempt further to postpone the board's decision. Thus, the election board at Hamburg cannot be blamed for finally appointing another organist at St. James's rather than Bach. This candidate even paid the 4000 marks to the church funds, as requested for the appointment. Bach's colleague at Hamburg, Johann Mattheson, a famous musician and musical writer, recalled this situation years later in his magazine, *'The Musical Patriot'*: *Besides some other untalented men, the son of a wealthy manual worker who was better at playing with money than with his fingers applied for the job, and was appointed organist.* Mattheson also told of the reaction of Erdmann Neumeister who gave vent in a Christmas sermon to his disappointment at not having the highly-respected Johann Sebastian Bach in his church: *This much is certain: Even if one of the angels of Bethlehem came down from heaven to play divine music and wanted to become organist at St. James's, but had no money, he could fly away.* Bach's half-hearted application leaves the impression that he was torn in various directions after the death of his wife, as would be expected of any man in such a situation. With Anna Magdalena, he found a new source of strength amidst the turmoil of life. New love, light, joy and a new enthusiasm for creating music returned.

We have no picture of Anna Magdalena

Bach. An oil-painting Carl Philipp Emanuel is recorded as having possessed has been lost. What kind of woman was she? She must have been extraordinarily robust - or she must have become robust during her marriage to Bach. References to her beautiful voice – Bach himself said that she *sang a very beautiful soprano* – may have been the inspiration for some authors, who have thought of her as a fragile, petite woman. The opposite must have been true. Her tender soul must have lived in a very strong body. Without such a robust physique, she would not have been able to bring up four stepchildren, bear thirteen children of her own, keep a huge household, make music and help her husband write down music. A number of Bach's works have been preserved only in copies by his wife. In the course of the years, Anna Magdalena's handwriting on the music manuscripts became so similar to that of her husband that for decades researchers considered her copies to be originals by Johann Sebastian. Only modern research methods, such as analysis of the paper and ink, have clarified this question. The observer who looks closely at the sheets of music written by this couple detects one of the most moving love stories in the literature of music – a love story in musical notes. However, there is something the observer can hardly see even with a magnifying glass. Only the camera brought it to light when we made a film about Bach: Anna Magdalena's handwriting often had more energetic and vigorous upstrokes and downward strokes, marks and notes; Johann Sebastian's handwriting seems to have been softer, even more tender, although he used a thicker quill and ink.

From today's viewpoint, Cöthen seems to have been a happy episode in Bach's life. Without these six years, the world of music would lack many of Bach's secular works. In the compositions he wrote at Cöthen, the

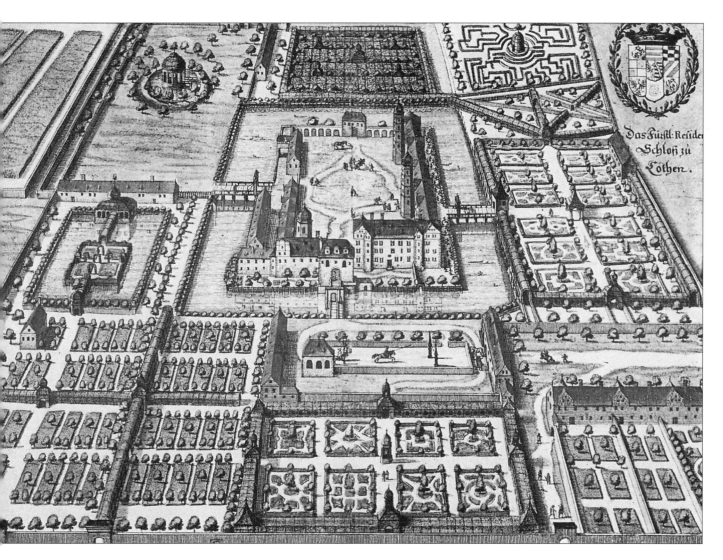

41. The royal castle at Cöthen. Engraving.

carefree, festive, happy atmosphere at court is reflected. Absent from the Calvinistic principality was the pious pettiness with which people of different denominations fought each other in so many 18th century towns. Prince Leopold's father had married a Protestant wife and demonstrated his generosity in matters of faith by allowing a Lutheran church and school. Bach's children probably attended this school. Prince Leopold proved his humane spirit by issuing an edict of toleration encouraging the members of the various denominations in his principality to respect one another. Thus, Bach could continue working at the organ, although the conditions at Cöthen were not ideal; there was no big organ in the town. He composed at least two secular cantatas each year: on the occasion of Leopold's birthday on December 10 and for New Year. For these cantatas, Bach used predominantly texts by Christian Friedrich Hunold, a poet who lived at nearby Halle, where he lectured on poetics and jurisprudence and wrote poems under the pseudonym 'Menantes'. Alfred Dürr writes:

Bach's celebratory cantatas at Cöthen were mostly 'serenatas.' A serenata was a kind of short opera with a modest dramatic action which could be performed theatrically, but a staged performance was not absolutely necessary. In most instances, there was merely talk of allegorical characters, gods or shep-

69

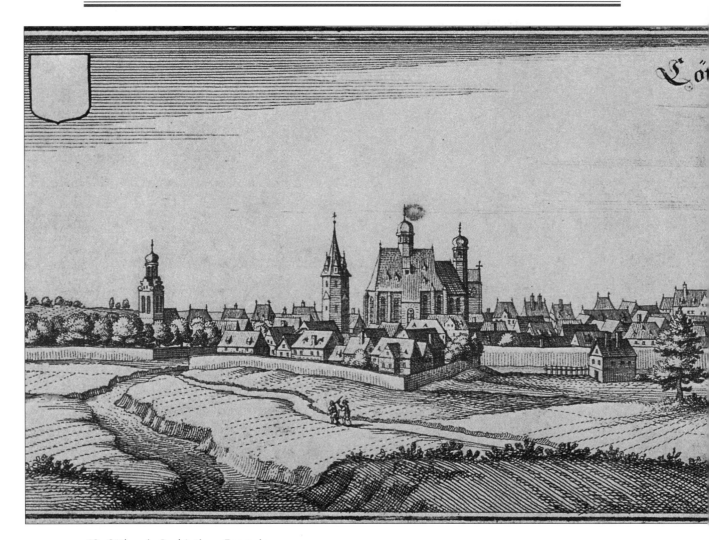

42. Cöthen in Bach's time. Engraving.

herds, who praised the qualities of their prince and at the end united in congratulating him. These secular works which he created occasionally adopted the happy tone of the poetic texts.

During Bach's years at Cöthen, instrumental works predominate. In no other period of his life did he compose instrumental works of such variety and richness. This shows the close influence on his activity as a composer by the place and purpose of making music. In the compositions Bach wrote for the royal court, French, Italian and German elements of style melded into a new kind of music typical of the baroque age. According to the instruments used in the respective pieces of music, Bach directed the performance from the harpsichord or viola, his two favourite instruments. The skills of individual members of the court orchestra also influenced his compositions. The archives at Cöthen give us the names, origin and instruments of the musicians who inspired Bach to compose his sonatas for violin, violoncello, gamba and flute. The violin concertos that are frequently performed today came into being at Cöthen, as well as the double concerto in D minor, the four great orchestral suites and – last but not least – the 'Six Concerts Avec Plusieurs Instruments' (Six Concerts With Several Instruments) as he himself entitled the Brandenburg Concertos. Margrave Christian

70

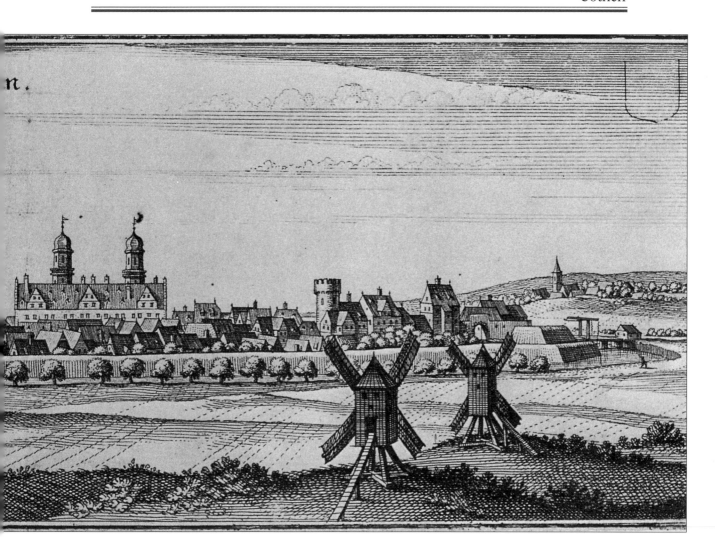

Ludwig of Brandenburg, a son of the Great Electoral Prince Frederick William of Prussia, commissioned them for his court orchestra at his castle in Berlin.

At Cöthen, Bach also composed numerous sonatas, toccatas, suites, fantasias, preludes and fugues for the clavier – a collective term for any keyboard instrument at that time. Bach's works at Cöthen attained the peak of court music and chamber music of the early 18th century. In none of these works do we meet the creative individualism which was antithetical to everyday music of the time but was later typical of Mozart, Beethoven and Schubert. Rather, a gifted court Kapellmeister and musician was reflecting the European musical trends of his time. It is no coinci-

dence that Bach increasingly copied, transcribed and changed compositions by other musicians. Probably only a fraction of these works have survived. They include compositions by Tommaso, Albinoni, Arcangelo Corelli, Girolamo Frescobaldi, Johann Jacob Froberger, Johann Caspar Kerll, Giovanni Legrenzi, Benedetto Marcello, Johann Adam Reincken, Georg Philipp Telemann and others whose works have their undisputed place in the repertoire of music, along with some who have been forgotten. Antonio Vivaldi's compositions greatly influenced Bach's orchestral works and as such occupy a dominant place in this list. Johann Mattheson describes the 'borrowing' of that time which was widespread and also characteristic of Bach:

43. Friederica Henrietta, Princess of Anhalt-Cöthen (1702-1723). Engraving.

Borrowing is not forbidden; but borrowed music must be paid back with interest. That means the copied music must be developed to create a more beautiful and better tone than the music it has been borrowed from.

Considering how composers such as Bach, Handel and Telemann 'borrowed' freely from each other in the 18th century, today's copyright law may be a positive achievement for the social and material security of the individual, but artistically such 'progress' is barren and rather ridiculous.

In his years at Cöthen, Bach also committed himself to another task which he had begun at Weimar, devoted to his growing number of children and students, including Anna Magdalena: composing and writing for didactic purposes. The first surviving evidence of this is the *'Little Organ Book'*, an annual cycle of choral preludes *in which a beginner at the organ is instructed how to*

perform a chorale in many ways and improve his pedalling by being forced to use the pedal when playing the chorales of this book. The next lines of the title page: *To the honour of Almighty God, and to the instruction of the neighbour. Author Johann Sebastian Bach, presently court Kapellmeister of His Majesty, the Prince of Anhalt-Cöthen.* Bach had probably begun working on this little organ book at Weimar. In January 1720, he started writing the *'Little Clavier Book for Wilhelm Friedemann Bach'* using the 63 piano pieces as lessons for his eldest son. In 1722, still at Cöthen, and in 1725, when he was in Leipzig, the two *'Little Clavier Books for Anna Magdalena Bach'* were written. The first booklet contained five

44. Leopold, Prince of Anhalt-Cöthen (1694-1728). Oil painting.

45. The hall of mirrors, Cöthen castle.

46. Johann Sebastian Bach as court Kapellmeister at Cöthen. Oil painting by Johann Jakob Ihle, c. 1720. The authenticity of the painting is disputed.

French suites and various short pieces, partly in Johann Sebastian's own handwriting, and partly in Anna Magdalena's. The second booklet, whose green vellum cover is adorned with the golden letters '*A.M.B. 1725*', contained numerous vocal and instrumental works, compositions by Bach himself and by others. Important and unimportant pieces were written side by side, documenting the everyday musical life of the Bach family. The entries were partly written by Bach, partly by his wife, and partly by his adolescent children. Thus, we can observe how Bach instructed his young wife and his many children in music and how he acquainted them with his own artistic intentions. The love song '*Willst du dein Herz mir schenken*' (Will you give me your heart) seems to have been just as characteristic of the couple as the chorale '*O Ewigkeit, du Donnerwort*' (O Eternity, you word of thunder) or the funeral song '*Schlummert ein, ihr matten*

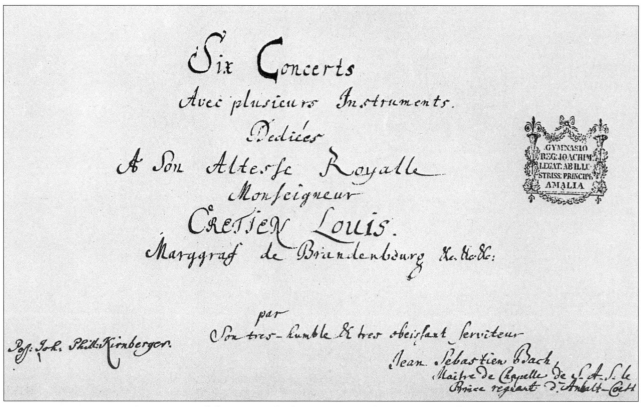

47. Autograph title page of the six Brandenburg Concertos (BWV 1046-1051).

Augen' (Fall asleep, you weary eyes). Death was a constant companion of this musical Bach family. Seven of the thirteen children Anna Magdalena bore died before their parents.

One of the teaching compositions Bach wrote during his time at Cöthen conquered a new land of music: *'The Well-Tempered Clavier.'* Bach wrote the First Part at Cöthen in 1722, the Second Part later in Leipzig (BWV 846-869). Although some musicians had tried to overcome the tuning problems of keyboard instruments before Bach, only Bach achieved the aim of a well-tempered tone – a well-balanced sound – with his collection of *'Preludes and Fugues Through All Tones and Semitones.'* Today's modern grand pianos are tuned in such a way that the distances between all the semitones are equal. In Bach's time, other tunings were preferred. The 24 keys were not equally usable; rather, the most usual keys were given a particularly

beautiful tone. In the two sets of 24 preludes and fugues of the two parts of the *'Well-Tempered Clavier,'* Bach developed a kind of tuning which was well balanced – *well-tempered* as he called it. Thus, certain differences in tone and sound characteristics of the individual keys remained, but for the first time all of them could be played very well. *To be used by talented young people who are eager to learn as well as by all those who already know how to play the clavier as a pastime*, as Bach wrote on the title page. The *'Well-Tempered Clavier'* – well-tempered tuning – became the basis for the development of European music from Bach via Classicism and Romanticism to today. Apart from the brilliant virtuosity of these pieces, even today's piano-tuners and pianists can best test their skills by the way they tune and interpret the *'Well-Tempered Clavier.'*

Two reasons have repeatedly been cited for Bach's departure from Anhalt-Cöthen. First

48. Christian Ludwig, Margrave of Brandenburg (1677-1734). Engraving.

of all, there was the *unmusical person*, as Bach called her – Princess Friederica Henrietta, née Princess of Anhalt-Berenburg, a cousin of Prince Leopold's, whom he married on December 11, 1721. The royal wedding took place one week after Bach's wedding to Anna Magdalena. The 19-year-old princess, who died only two years later, even before Bach left Cöthen, and the court

Kapellmeister, do not seem greatly to have liked one another. On October 28, 1730, Bach wrote, remembering his time at Cöthen:

There I had a generous prince who loved and appreciated music; I even thought I could spend the rest of my life at his court. But it so happened that this prince married a princess of Berenburg and the musical inclination of the prince seemed to diminish, par-

77

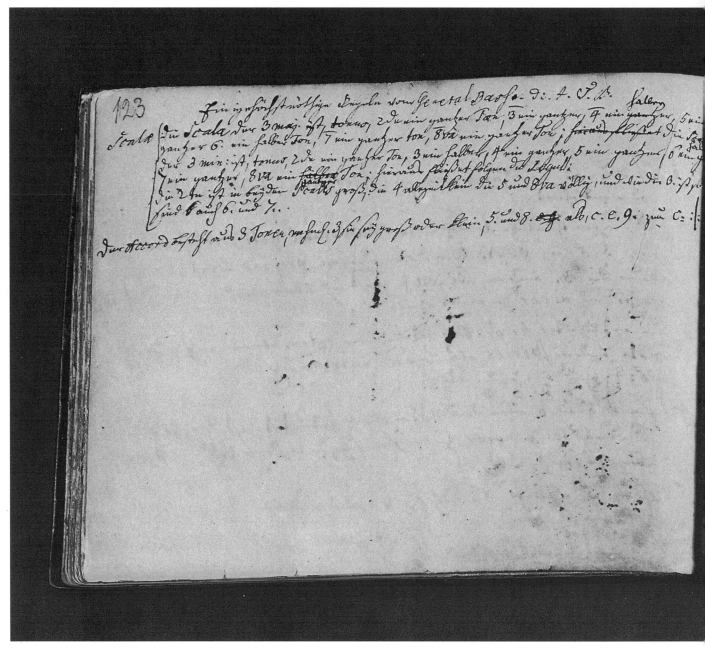

49. The second '*Little Clavier Book for Anna Magdalena Bach*', 1725. *Left*, an entry by her son Johann Christoph Friedrich; *right*, the handwriting of his mother Anna Magdalena. Johann Sebastian Bach probably gave instructions to both entries about the basso continuo.

ticularly since the new princess seemed to be an unmusical person.

However, it is probably wrong to overemphasize the influence of the young *unmusical person* on Bach's decision to look for another field of activity. The major reason was Bach's desire to commit himself to church music – his *ultimate aim, a well-regulated church*

music for God's honour. Another reason was the fact that his *sons seemed to be inclined to study*, as he wrote – they seem to have wanted to attend university, and at Cöthen there was none. Thus, Bach's interest was drawn to nearby Leipzig. Prince Leopold did not try to hold him back. In his letter of dismissal dated from April 13, 1723, he stressed

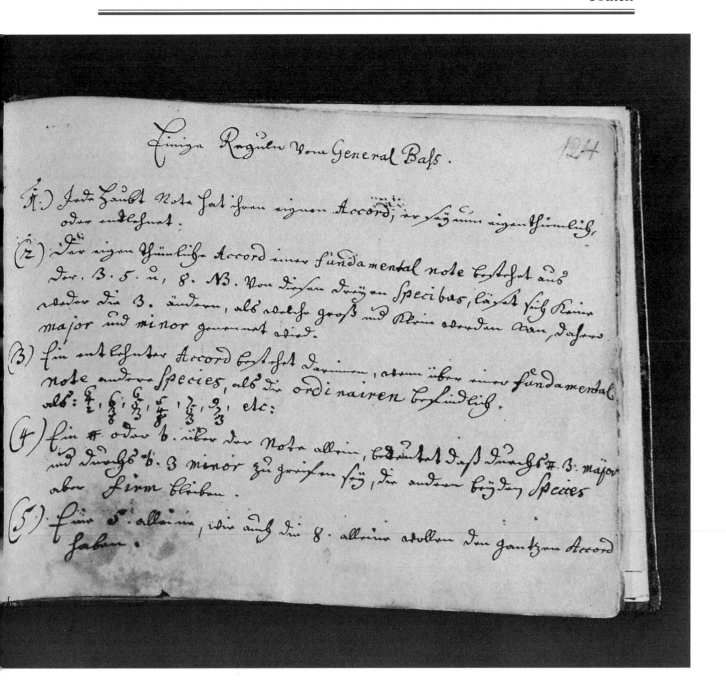

that he *was always very content with Bach's work* and *could recommend him for other service*. They remained friends. Bach and his wife often returned to Cöthen and played and sang at the court. In the following years, generous fees for guest performances for both of them were recorded in the archives of Cöthen under the heading: *To the Cantor of Leipzig, Bach, and to his wife who could often be listened to at Cöthen.*

Prince Leopold of Anhalt-Cöthen died on November 19, 1728, at the age of 34. The requiem Bach dedicated to his greatest patron has been lost. Only the text has been preserved: *Complain, children, complain to all the world.*

Bach becomes Cantor of St. Thomas's

In the musical life of central and northern Germany, two cities attracted every church musician in 1723: Hamburg and Leipzig. Hamburg's churches were famous for their great organs. At the end of the 17th and at the beginning of the 18th century, Dietrich Buxtehude was a frequent guest in the city. In 1722, the famous Reincken died in Hamburg – a year before his hundredth birthday. Since 1715, Erdmann Neumeister had been senior

50. Autograph of the B minor partita for violin (BWV 1002).

pastor at St. James's church. In 1721, Telemann took up the envied post of Hamburg's musical director. From an historical point of view, Erdmann Neumeister's unsuccessful attempt to make Bach come to Hamburg had a significance that he and his contemporaries could not have fathomed at the time. But if we look at Bach's years at Cöthen, the compositions he wrote there and the change in his life when he married Anna Magdalena, it can also be regarded as a vagary of fate that no suitable post was vacant for Bach in Hamburg.

In Leipzig, things were completely different.

Here too there was a great tradition of church music. Since the foundation of the Augustinian monastery of St. Thomas in the year 1212, young clergymen – students of the monastery school – made church music in Leipzig. They were the predecessors of the St Thomas choir that was formed years later. After the triumph of the Reformation, the Leipzig city council bought the monastery of St. Thomas and also took over the patronage of St. Thomas's school. St. Thomas's and the adjoining school became the musical centre of the city. The Cantor of St. Thomas's was

51. The same in a copy by Anna Magdalena.

the musical director of the city, and was also responsible for music at the main city church, St. Nikolai, at two other churches, and for church music at the university.

When in June 1722, the Cantor of St. Thomas's, Leipzig, Johann Kuhnau, a respected scholar and composer of clavier works, died, many church musicians looked to Leipzig – as did Bach. But initially he seemed to stand no chance. The city council immediately contacted Telemann, who had studied law in Leipzig, had been director of the musical college he himself had founded at the university, and worked as organist at the New Church. Many people in Leipzig remembered him very positively. Invited by the council, Telemann came to Leipzig on August 1. On August 9, he gave his trial performance, which was officially required, playing a cantata, and was elected Cantor of St. Thomas's on August 12. The next day the council formally informed him of his election and handed him the contract of employment, with the special conditions that had been negotiated. Then Telemann returned to Hamburg, where he handed in his letter of resignation to his employers on September 3. What happened then can only be guessed. In any case, Telemann turned down the offer by Leipzig city council in a letter, after having delayed for some time and after his employers in Hamburg had offered to increase his salary.

In the council's minutes dated December 21, 1722, there is a note that *several others had applied for the job, among them Kapellmeister Graupner from Darmstadt and Bach from Cöthen.* Court Kapellmeister Christoph Graupner was also well known in Leipzig, and was two years senior to Bach. He had attended St. Thomas's school, studied law in Leipzig, like Telemann, and learned composition from Kuhnau. After staying in Hamburg for a short time, he had entered the

service of the Landgrave of Hesse at Darmstadt, where he wrote many operas, piano pieces and much chamber music. His reputation as a composer quickly spread among his contemporaries, not least due to the sheer quantity of his works; 1,300 cantatas, 116 symphonies and 130 concertos and overtures are still extant. Graupner was more famous than Bach and was well-known by the people of Leipzig. It is no wonder that the council preferred him. But after their disappointment with Telemann, they prudently did not turn down the other eight applicants. On January 1723, Graupner gave his trial performance. Then he returned to his employer at Darmstadt with a letter from the Leipzig council asking for his release. But the landgrave refused to release Graupner, and increased his salary. On April 22, Graupner informed the council that he had withdrawn his application. Thus, Bach and two other applicants came to the top of the list. The words of the influential senior mayor of Leipzig and city councillor, Abraham Christoph Platz, at the council's meeting on April 9, reflected the attitude of the council: *Since we cannot get the best, we have to make do with a mediocrity.*

But it would be wrong to accuse the Leipzig councillors of being philistines. Although Bach was a respected organist and court Kapellmeister, he was not yet known as a composer of church cantatas. The cantatas he had created at Weimar were unknown in Leipzig. And the main job of the new Cantor of St. Thomas's was to write cantatas for the church's year. Besides, Bach had not attended university, like his predecessors at St. Thomas's. Usually a degree was needed for teaching at St. Thomas's school, one of the Cantor's duties. After Telemann and Graupner had declined their offer, the councillors' major concern was that Bach and the other two applicants *perhaps could not*

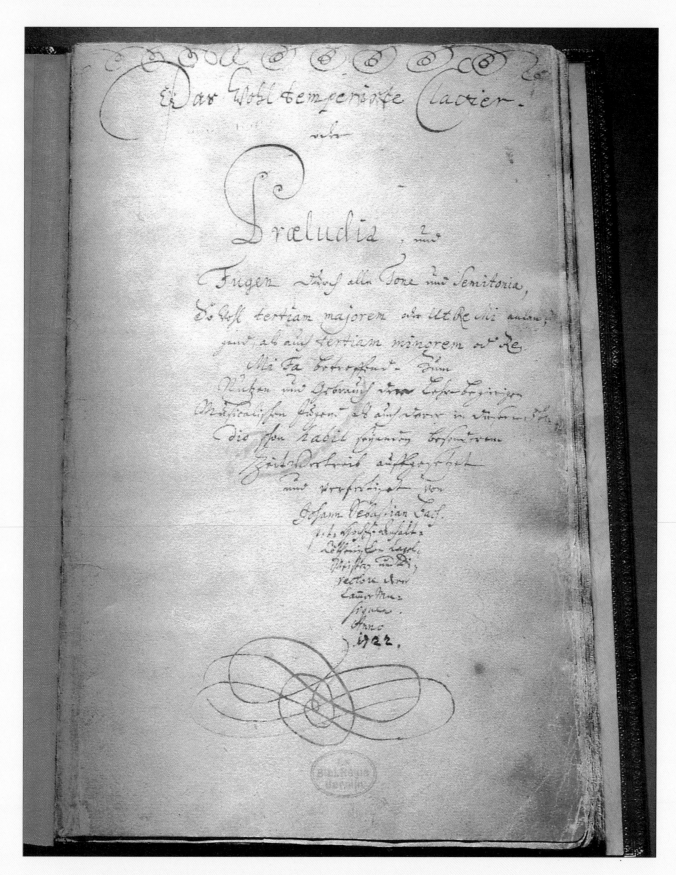

52. Autograph title page of 'The Well-Tempered Clavier' (BWV 846-869).

inform. 'Informing' was another word for teaching. However, the Leipzig city council seems to have treated the court Kapellmeister of Cöthen, Johann Sebastian Bach, with more respect than the two other applicants: Bach's travelling expenses to Leipzig were reimbursed, those of the other applicants were not. Moreover the councillors seem very quickly to have stopped hesitating and decided in Bach's favour. At Cöthen, Bach had composed the cantata *'Du wahrer Gott und Davids Sohn'* ('You true God and David's son;' BWV 23) for his Leipzig application. Whether he played this cantata at his trial performance is not known. However, a copy of a partita from his second trial cantata survives, written by Johann Andreas Kuhnau, a student at St. Thomas's and a nephew of the late Cantor, with the comment *This was the trial performance in Leipzig*. This cantata, *'Jesus nahm zu sich die Zwölfe'* (Jesus took to him the Twelve; BWV 22), must have been the composition referred to in the chronicle by Riemer: *The 7th Sunday, Esto Mihi, Mr Sebastian Bach, Kapellmeister at Cöthen at the time, gave his trial performance applying for the vacant Cantorate at St. Thomas's after the death of the late Mr Kuhnau.* A newspaper report in Hamburg's 'Relationscourier' dated Leipzig, February 9 said of Bach's trial performance: *The music he played on that occasion was much praised by all those who appreciate art.* Certainly some councillors also attended this trial performance on Sunday. News of Bach's skill must have reached the 32 council members. On April 22, 1723, Bach was unanimously elected Cantor of St. Thomas's. 29 of the 32 councillors – including all three mayors – were present when the election took place. The minutes of the council meeting concluded: *It would be necessary to try to secure a famous man in order to motivate the students. Bach has to ask for his dis-*

missal, and he is hopeful that his wish will be granted. Thus, this consultation found an end. After this, Bach had to undergo a test on the Articles of Faith by the church council and was sworn in on the formula of concords. The latter was necessary for the church authorities to recognize the election. Then Bach's superior in church, superintendent Deyling, received the formal confirmation of the election by the council, asking him *to give the elected Bach the necessary instructions for his job.*

Such a procedure for electing the Cantor shows the close interdependence of secular and clerical power in Bach's time. Of course, tensions, rivalries, even personal enmities between secular and spiritual dignitaries were inevitable in such a relationship. Besides, in cities like Leipzig, the leading citizens had a strong desire to avoid clerical domination. However, a man who was employed by the city, such as the Cantor of St. Thomas's, had first of all to fulfil his musical duties within the church and, therefore, could only be employed with the explicit agreement of the church authorities. Therefore, the final decision was made by the church. Before the Age of Enlightenment there was no separation between secular and clerical power, such as is today taken for granted.

The lengthy procedure before he was finally elected Cantor at St. Thomas's may be one reason why years later Bach spoke of this appointment without enthusiasm. He wrote about it in a letter dated October 28, 1730, to Georg Erdmann, a friend since childhood – they attended school together at Ohrdruf and later at Lüneburg. At this time, Erdmann was Court Councillor in the service of the Russian Emperor at Gdansk. He received the only surviving letter in which Bach speaks of his career and private life:

So God made it possible for me to be appointed musical director and Cantor at St.

Templum S. Jacobi. | St. Iakobskerk, waar van de Toren vervaerdigt is in 't Iaar 1580. Synde de Kerk, daar de beroemde Doctor Meier in predikt.

et Schenk exc. Amstold c.P.

53. The church of St. James, Hamburg. Engraving published by Peter Schenk, Amsterdam, c. 1700.

Thomas's school, Leipzig. Although at first it did not seem any improvement to leave the post of a Kapellmeister and become a Cantor – and it took three months to make this decision – this job was described very favourably to me (besides, my sons seemed to be inclined to study). Thus, in the name of the Lord, I dared to go to Leipzig, gave my trial performance and finally moved here.

In the contemporary social hierarchy, the title and position of court Kapellmeister was generally more respected than that of Cantor. But Bach knew very well that the Cantor of St. Thomas's, Leipzig could not be compared to Cantors at other churches.

On May 29, 1723, the *'National Scholars' Magazine of the Neutral Correspondent of Holstein'* – one of the few national magazines of the time – reported from Leipzig:

Last Saturday around noon, four coaches with household equipment arrived from Cöthen. They belonged to the former royal

85

54. Erdmann Neumeister (1671-1756). Engraving by Christian Fritzsch, 1719.

court Kapellmeister who was called to Leipzig and appointed Cantor at St. Thomas's. At two o'clock he and his family arrived in two coaches and moved into the newly renovated apartment at St. Thomas's school.

Bach's future duties were laid down in an extensive *Contract* which he had to sign after being elected:

55. Hamburg at the end of the 17th/beginning of the 18th century.

Contract of Employment as the Cantor of St. Thomas's.

Whereas the Honourable and Most Wise Council of the City of Leipzig have appointed me Cantor of St. Thomas's School and asked me to sign a contract concerning the following matters:

1. That my life will be a good example to the boys at the schools, and will be committed loyally to teaching and informing them.

2. That I will make music in the two major city churches as well as I can.

3. That I will accord the Honourable and Most Wise Council all due respect and will obey their instructions and observe and support their honour and reputation everywhere as far as I can. And if any Councillor asks the boys to make music, this will be done without hesitation. Except with the consent of the ruling Mayor and Headmasters of the schools, they will never leave the city to make music at funerals or at weddings.

4. That I will obey any instructions given by the Superintendents and Headmasters of the schools concerning anything they order in the name of the Honourable and Most Wise Council.

5. That I will not accept any boys who have not

56. The church of St. Thomas, Leipzig. Engraving by G. Bodenehr the Elder.

57. Georg Philipp Telemann (1681-1767). Engraving by G. Lichtensteger.

yet had basic instruction in music, or at least are talented in music, so that they can be instructed in this art, and that I will not do anything of this nature without informing the Superintendents and Headmasters beforehand and asking their consent.

6. That I will instruct the boys both in vocal and instrumental music so that unnecessary costs for the churches can be avoided.

7. That in order to maintain good order in the church, I will perform music in such a way that it will not take too much time and not sound like an opera but rather encourage the listeners to pray and worship God.

8. That I will provide the new church with good students.

9. That I will deal with the boys in a friendly manner, but if they do not want to obey orders, I will discipline them with moderation or inform the Authorities responsible.

10. That I will carry out the instruction at school and anything else I have to do in a loyal way.

11. And that I will ask another person to do so if I am not able to do so myself, without receiving financial support by your Honourable and Most Wise Council or the school.

12. That I will not leave town without the Mayor's permission.

13. That I will accompany the boys at funerals as far as possible.

14. And that I will not accept any post at the university without the Honourable and Respected Council's permission.

I hereby commit myself truly and loyally to keep all the provisions mentioned above, and I will not break these rules knowing that I might otherwise lose my position.

I signed this contract with my own hand and confirmed it with my own seal. This was done in Leipzig on May 5, 1723.

Johann Sebastian Bach

1. Arx Pleissenburg. 2. Porta S. Petri. 3. Templ. S. Petri. 4. Domus Provisionis. 5.
Hortus Bosianus. 6. Templ. S. Thomæ. 7. Domus Pañar. 8. Templ. Minorit.
sive Templ. novam. 9. Turriculus Curiæ. 10. Templ. et Colleg. S. Pauli. 11. Porta
Grimiana. 12. Templ. S. Nicolai. 13. S. Johan. sive Templ. Coemeterii. 14. Xenodo-
chium opulentia præcipuum. 15. Ergastulum et orphanotrophium.

1. Die Vestung Weissenburg. 2. das Peters thor. 3. S. Peters kirch. 4. Proviant Haus
5. Bosens Garten. 6. S. Thomas kirch. 7. das Gewand-Haus. 8. die Parfisser oder
neue kirch. 9. das Rath-Haus thürn. 10. die Paudiner kirch u. Collegium. 11. das Grim
mische Thor. 12. die S. Nicolaus kirch. 13. S. Johans od' Begräbnis kirch. 14. das
Reiche Spittal. 15. das Zucht u. Waisen-Haus.

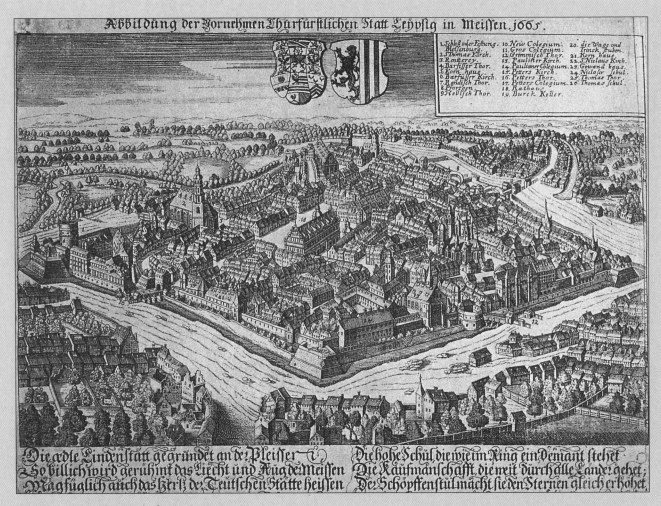

59. The electoral capital of Leipzig. Engraving.

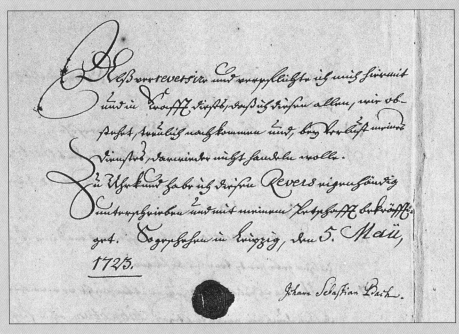

60. Page 4 of the contract, with Bach's signature.

58. Leipzig c. 1720. Coloured engraving by Johann Georg Ringlin, according to Friedrich Bernhard Werner.

61. The Bible of the city of Leipzig upon which Bach is believed to have taken his oath of office.

Das RATH-HAUS und
Der Grosse MARCK in LEIPZIG.

1. Das Rath Hauß.
2. Der Grosse Marck.
3. Kramläden unter dem Rathhauß.
4. Die Acciß.
5. Roth Haupts Hoff.
6. Die Heü Straß.
7. Der Raths Keller.
8. Ein Schöpff brunn.
9. Die Katter Stras.
10. Saltz gæssichen.

Gabriel Bodenehr ad vivum del. et Excud.
Cum Gratia et Priv. Sac. Cæs. Majest.

62. The city hall and the Great Market of Leipzig. Engraving by Gabriel Bodenehr the Elder.

The situation in the city of Leipzig was totally different from that in the principality of Cöthen. No young, musical prince, whose tolerance was widely known and who admired his court Kapellmeister, ruled in Leipzig, but a clumsy board of citizens. Their decisions and resolutions were executed bureaucratically in the city offices. When Bach moved to Leipzig, this meant another new beginning for the 38-year-old composer – with new people, new opportunities and new problems. He had a foretaste of this new life when he was ceremonially installed in his office at St. Thomas's school on June 1. The rector, teachers, pupils and choirboys of St. Thomas's gathered for the ceremony. Two representatives of the council and the pastor of St. Thomas's, representing the church board, lent official dignity to the ceremony –

and immediately began quarrelling. The representatives of the council accused the pastor, who was also the superintendent of the schools of St. Thomas's, of having spoken words of greeting and encouragement to Bach which were the prerogative of the city council and not the church board. It was apparently only out of consideration for the pupils who were present that the dignitaries refrained from starting a public argument. Records of the struggle for competence, even joined by the superintendent years later, filled many pages. Tensions like those between the two authorities who employed him often fuelled Bach's aspirations for independence. He made use of their disagreements and sometimes even fanned their flames.

63. Bach's letter to Georg Erdmann, dated October 28, 1730.

HochEdelgebohrner Herr.

Ewr. HochEdelgeb. werden einen alten treuen
Diener deßwegen excusiren, daß er sich die Frey-
heit einmal Ihnen mit diesen zu incommo-
diren. Es werden nunmehr fast 2 Jahr ver-
floßen seyn, da E. HochEdelgeb. auf mein an
Ihnen abgelaßenes mit einer gütigen Ant-
wort beglückten, kaum muß das außern,
daß Ihnen wegen meiner fatalitäten einige
Nachricht zu geben, so zugleich verlanget
wurde, als soll solches hiermit gehorsamst
erstattet werden. Von Jugend auf sind
Ihnen meine fata bekannt bis ietzt, biß auf
die mutation so mich als Capellmeister
nach Löffen zog. Daselbst hatte einen
gnädigen und Music so hoch liebenden als
kennenden Fürsten, bey dessen Leben auch ver-
meinte meine Lebenszeit zu beschließen.
Es mußte sich aber fügen, daß erwehnter Herr
nachdem sich mit einer Berenburgisch Prin-
ceßin vermählete, da es dann das Ansehen
gewinnen wolte, als ob die musicalische

Life in Leipzig

The city of Leipzig had some 25,000 inhabitants when Bach moved there in 1723. Within the city walls, which had been built in the Middle Ages, there lived a self-confident bourgeoisie, made up of merchants and manual workers. The social structure of the population was more balanced than in other cities of the time. This may have been due to its money, but also to the city's good, thrifty administration. Leipzig was one of the most important trading centres of Europe at that time. Every year three fairs took place at Leipzig, attracting many foreigners. The court of Frederick Augustus I in Dresden was the political and artistic centre of the Electorate of Saxony, and Leipzig its economic centre. The Prince Elector of Saxony was also King of Poland. Saxony's industrial products and merchandise were exported via Leipzig to eastern Europe, and agricultural products and raw materials from Poland imported into Germany. The inhabitants of Leipzig knew how to count the pennies. A conservative business sense existed in the city alongside a pious Lutheran tradition. In this city, Dr Martin Luther had his famous successful dispute with his greatest theological opponent, the Catholic professor Dr Johann Eckstein, from Ingolstadt in Bavaria. The citizens were as proud of this historic dispute as they were of their impressive city hall, Great Market and the rich town houses surrounding it. The church and school of St. Thomas were close in more than geographical terms to this famous city hall, the stock exchange and the castle cellar.

Those who wanted to be successful in Leipzig had to be on good terms both with the powerful bourgeoisie and with the Almighty. They were permitted to have some disputes with the rich and the powerful, as Bach had several times. They were no dictators, nor were they philistines. But he had to become one of them. The city was ruled by the so-called 'three councils' as the full council committee, which only met on important occasions, was called. The election of the new Cantor of St. Thomas's was one such occasion. In 1723 there were 32 councillors, elected for life; among them were the three mayors, each of whom presided at one of the three councils. One of the three councils was called 'the sitting council', which virtually managed the administration. The other two councils were called 'the resting councils.' The three councils took turns to manage the administration. If decisions exceeded the authority of a single council, but were not important enough to gather all three councils, the so-called 'select council' met, consisting of the oldest members of all three councils. In the records it is referred to as 'the select one.' At least among the three dozen councillors there was a democratic form of administration. The citizens also benefited from this constellation. Being on bad terms with one mayor or councillor did not mean being on bad terms with the entire council. The citizens seem to have been adept at playing off the men in power against one another whenever they wanted to. As was Bach.

The council's majority was sometimes against Bach; the reason for this was not so much the intolerance of the councillors as

64. Street map of Leipzig.

Bach's independence, even stubbornness. Like many great artists, he considered his own problems possessed a high priority, which naturally they did not do for the councillors. Since Bach was sensitive and easily hurt, conflicts with the council were inevitable. These conflicts have often been overestimated. Those responsible for administering the community sometimes have to give everyday concerns priority over art. They are not necessarily unmusical philistines. This is also true of the Leipzig councillors of Bach's time, who have often come in for criticism.

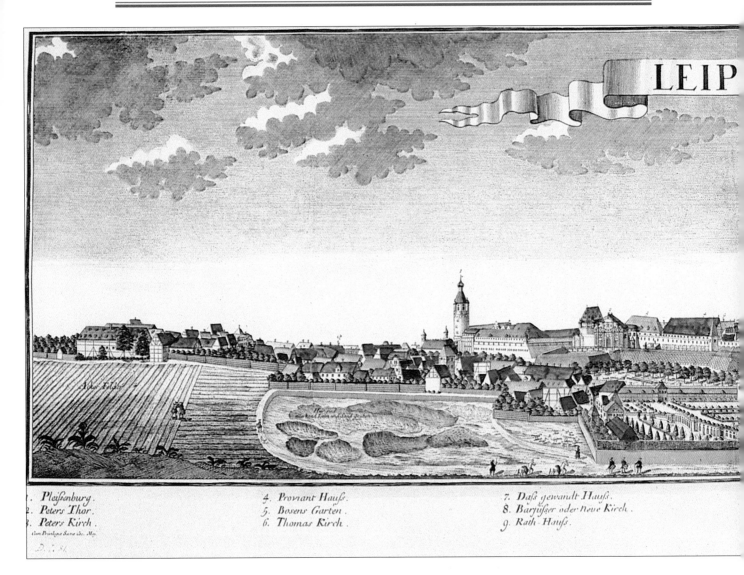

LEIP

1. *Pleißenburg*.
2. *Peters Thor*.
3. *Peters Kirch*.

4. *Proviant Hauß*.
5. *Bosens Garten*.
6. *Thomas Kirch*.

7. *Daß gewandt Hauß*.
8. *Barfüßer oder Neue Kirch*.
9. *Rath-Hauß*.

65. Prospect of Leipzig. Coloured engraving by Friedrich Bernhard Werner.

In the council, every respected profession and craft was represented: generals, judges, architects, university professors, ministers, landlords, senior city clerks, merchants and other respected citizens. One of them always served as headmaster of St. Thomas's school. In the course of the years, Bach risked uttering some highly emotive and critical words against the city authorities of Leipzig, did not shy away from conflicts, and repeatedly incurred the displeasure of his municipal superiors in his function as teacher. Individual councillors reacted in different ways to his obstinacy, depending on their personal sympathy and musicality. But despite all the conflicts, Bach's attempts to reach an agreement with the dignitaries at Leipzig, the cleverness with which he proceeded, and the councillors' willingness to come to terms with the self-confident Cantor and musical director, are indisputable. Bach also knew how to gain respect in Leipzig. He became increasingly famous, even an institution in Leipzig, inseparable from the city's life.

Some councillors and their families soon became friends of the Bachs. This is reflected in the names of the godfathers of Bach's chil-

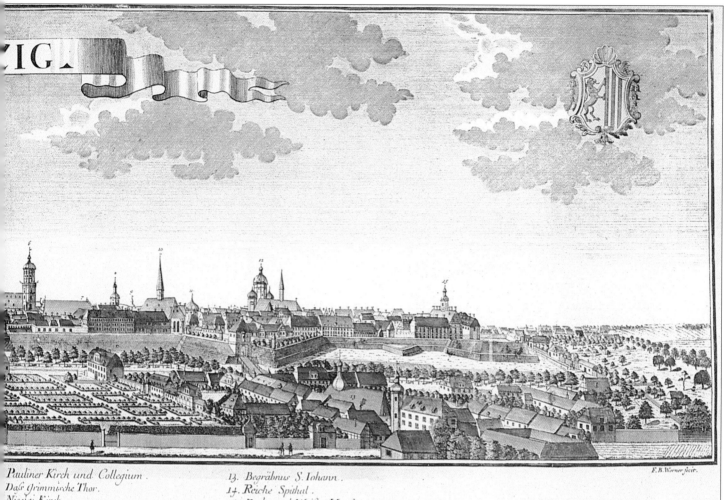

Pauliner Kirch und Collegium.
Dass Grimmische Thor.
Nicolai Kirch.

13. Begräbnus S. Iohann.
14. Reiche Spithal.
15. Zucht und Waisen Hauss.

F. B. Werner fecit.

66. The city of Leipzig with the market and city hall. Engraving by Johann Georg Schreiber, 1712 (*overleaf*).

dren, and also in the commissions for compositions. In his letter to Georg Erdmann, Bach told of his remarkable income in Leipzig. It varied according to the number of weddings, funerals and other occasional jobs that increased the annual income of the Cantor.

My present income is about 700 thalers, and if there are more funerals, my additional income rises; but if everyone is healthy, there are not so many funerals. Last year, I earned 100 thalers less than usual due to this fact.

In this same letter, Bach complained that he would be able to live a better life in Thuringia with 400 thalers than in Leipzig with double the sum. This complaint is understandable if one considers his situation in October 1730. The disagreements with the Leipzig Council had just reached their climax, after Bach's complaint about the inadequate funding of church music. Bach wanted to leave Leipzig, and wanted Erdmann to help him find another position.

Bach's life in Leipzig for three decades reflected the normal range of human emotions found in all our lives – the ups and downs, anger and joy, injustices he had to suffer and injustices he brought upon him-

99

Erklärung der Nummern.

1 Das Rath-Hauß.
2 Die Brimsche Gaße.
3 Die Peter-Straße.
4 Das Thomas Gäßgen.
5 Das Baarfüsser Gäßgen.
6 Die Hen Straße.
7 Die Lather Straße.
8 Das Saltz Gäßgen.
9 Die Börse.
10 Der Börsen oder fisch Marckt.
11 Die Brod Bäncke.
12 Die fleisch Bäncke.
13 Die Reichs Straße.
14 Das Schuster Gäßgen.
15 Die Nidaus Straße.
16 Das Holdhan Gäßgen.
17 Die Nidaus Kirche.
18 Die Ritter Straße.

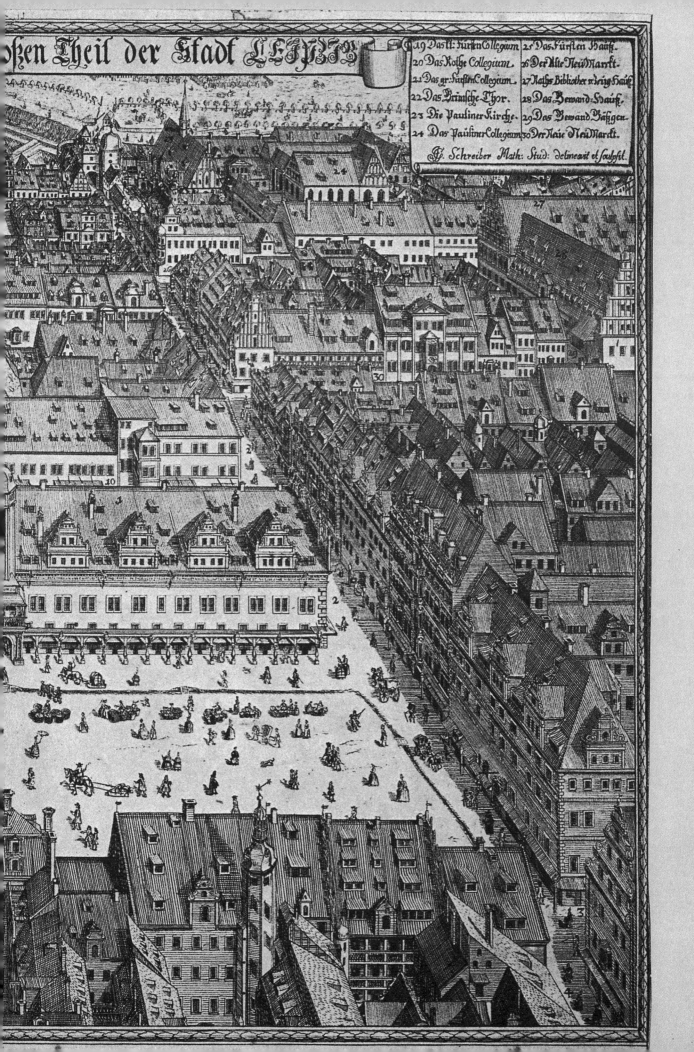

...ßen Theil der Stadt LEIPZIG

19 Das II. Fürsten Collegium.   25 Das Fürsten Hauß.
20 Das Rothe Collegium.   26 Der Alte Neü Marckt.
21 Das gr. Fürsten Collegium.   27 Raths Bibliothec u. Zeug Hauß.
22 Das Grimische Thor.   28 Das Gewand Hauß.
23 Die Pauliner Kirche.   29 Das Gewand Gäßgen.
24 Das Pauliner Collegium.   30 Der Neüe Neü Marckt.

G. Schreiber Math: Stud: delineavit et sculpsit.

67.

68.

The six mayors of the city of Leipzig during Bach's 27 years' service in the city (nos. 67-72), and eight councillors (nos. 73-80) who participated in Bach's election to become Cantor at St. Thomas's. Engravings by Martin Bernigeroth (1670-1733) and Johann Martin Bernigeroth (1713-1767).

67. Abraham Christoph Platz (1658-1728).

68. Jacob Born (1683-1758).

69. Gottfried Wilhelm Küstner (1689-1762).

70. Gottfried Lange (1672-1748).

71. Christian Ludwig Stieglitz (1677-1758).

72. Adrian Steger (1662-1741).

73. Johann Ernst Kregel von Sternbach (1652-1731).

74. Carl Friedrich Trier (1690-1763).

75. Gottfried Conrad Lehmann (1661-1728).

76. Gottfried Winkler (1684-1740).

77. Johann Franciscus Born (1669-1732).

78. Theodor Örtel (1659-1734).

79. Johann Jacob Mascov (1689-1761).

80. Gottfried Wagner (1652-1740).

69.

70.

71.

72.

73.

74.

75.

76.

77.

78.

79.

80.

81. The castle cellar, stock exchange and city hall, Leipzig. Engraving.

self, criticism and recognition of his work. This was all part of Bach's existence just as much as the timeless music he composed as an everyday duty. One of the things that angered Bach seems to have been the fact that some mean but wealthy Leipzigers married, or had their children married, in nearby village churches to cheat the Cantor of St. Thomas's and his musicians of their fees for the celebration. In summer 1733, Bach, together with the organist of St. Thomas's and the rector of the school (who represented the students in their claim for fees) appealed to the city council:

Your Honourable and Highly Respected Sirs and Patrons, we hereby inform you of the fact that Mr Johann Friedrich Eitelwein, merchant in Leipzig, celebrated his wedding outside of Leipzig on 12 August of this year and seemed to consider it his right to cheat us in this case of our fees and refused to pay us the money even after being reminded of it several times . . . Thus we are forced to ask your Honourable and Highly Respected Sirs

and Patrons, to protect us in this affair.

And in a letter *To the Electoral Consistory of Saxony in Leipzig* they wrote: *Thus, we appeal to the justice and friendship of your Honourable and Most Wise Gentlemen and Patrons and humbly ask you to protect us and assist us to receive the income we need for our daily lives.*

Every year, a new Bach child was born. From 1723 to 1733, the year of the letter mentioned above, ten children were born. Bach had to count the pennies, and he was good at doing so. He was able to provide well for himself and for his family in Leipzig; his children received the tuition appropriate to their social standing. Within the circle of the well-heeled citizens of Leipzig, whom he met every day, the former court Kapellmeister at Anhalt-Cöthen became the self-confident burgher Johann Sebastian Bach. He loved good meals, he liked to drink a good glass of wine now and then, and he enjoyed drinking coffee, which he even praised in a cantata: '*Schweigt stille, plaudert nicht*' (Be quiet, do

106

82. Johann Sebastian Bach. A pastel picture by Gottlieb Friedrich Bach, around 1736 (or by Johann Philipp Bach, around 1780). The picture may have been painted after Bach's death.

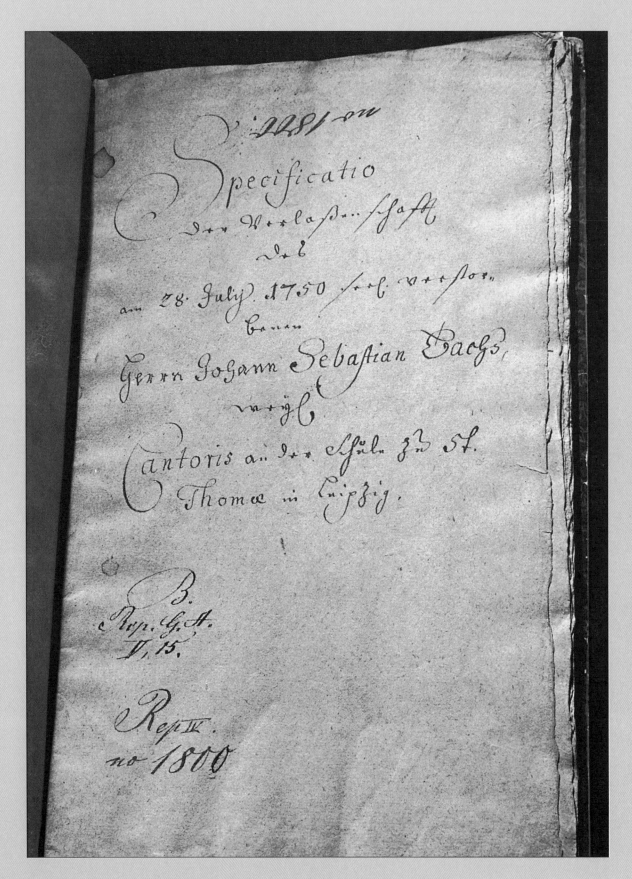

83. Inventory of Johann Sebastian Bach's estate. Leipzig, autumn 1750.

	Nₜ	H	₰

Cap. VI.
In Instrumenten.

1. fourniral Clavecin, welcher bey der Familie, so viel mög: lich bleiben soll	80	—	—
	50	—	—
1. Clavesin	50	—	—
1. dito	50	—	—
2. dito	20	—	—
1. dito kleiner	30	—	—
1. Lauten Werck	30	—	—
1. dito	8	—	—
1. Steinerische Violine	2	—	—
1. schlechtere violine	1	8	—
1. dito Piccolo	—	5	—
1. Braccie	—	5	—
1. dito	—	16	—
1. dito	6	—	—
1. Bassettgen	6	—	—
1. Violoncello	—	16	—
1. dito	3	—	—
1. viola da Gamba			

84. List of the musical instruments in Bach's estate.

Kurtzer, iedoch höchstnöthiger Entwurff
einer Wohlbestallten Kirchen Music; nebst
einigem unvorgreiflichen Bedencken, von
dem Verfall derselben.

Zu einer Wohlbestallten Kirchen Music gehören
Vocalisten und Instrumentisten.
Die Vocalisten werden hiesiges Ortes von denen
Thomas Schülern formiret, und zwar von 4erley
Sorten, als Discantisten, Altisten, Tenoristen
und Bassisten.
So nun die Chöre derer Kirchen Stücke recht, wie
es sich gebühret, bestallt werden sollen, müßen
die Vocalisten wiederum in 2erley Sorten
eingetheilet werden, als: Concertisten und
Ripienisten.
Derer Concertisten sind ordinaire 4; auch
wohl 5, 6, 7 biß 8; so man nemlich per Choros
musiciren will.
Derer Ripienisten müßen wenigstens auch
achte seyn, nemlich zu ieder Stimme 2.
Die Instrumentisten werden auch in unterschie-
dene Arten eingetheilet, als: Violisten,
Hautboisten, Fleutenisten, Trompetter
und Paucken. NB. Zu denen Violisten

85. Bach's petition to Leipzig city council, dated 23 August, 1730.

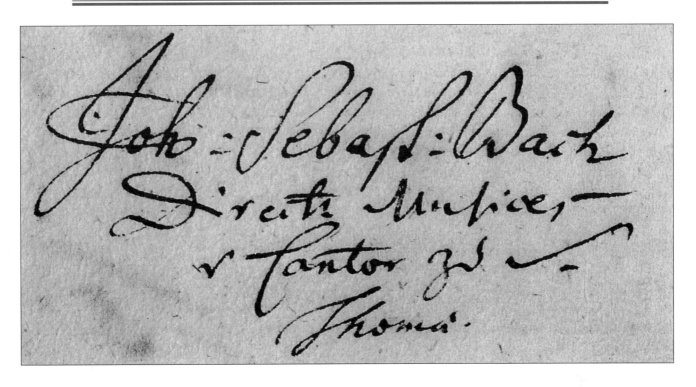

86. Bach's signature.

not talk; BWV 211) – the so-called Coffee Cantata. He knew the value of money, and he knew how to save it. In spite of the expenses for his large family, as well as for a maid and guests of the family, he even became modestly prosperous. The official list of his estate included mining shares, money, gold and silver coins, silver utensils and other precious things, 19 musical instruments, household equipment made of pewter, copper and bronze, as well as furniture, clothes and his theological library. The entire value of his estate could be estimated at £30,000. If the instruments were valued at today's prices, this sum would be even higher.

When Bach fought for money, he did so not only because of its material value. His reputation, as well as the conditions for his musical work, were major concerns when he argued with the university of Leipzig for several years. He fought ostensibly for the 12 gulden a year his predecessors as Cantors at St. Thomas's had been paid for their service at St. Paul's church, the university church.

After Kuhnau's death, the university stopped paying these 12 gulden. But in reality, this was a fight about authority. From the outset, Bach considered himself 'director of music' – the director of the entire church music of Leipzig. The university authorities did not accept this claim, least of all the organist of the university, Johann Gottlieb Görner. Görner had been a student at St. Thomas's since 1712, became organist at St. Paul's church in 1716, and in 1721 organist of the main city church, St. Nikolai's. After Kuhnau's death, Görner also fulfilled his Cantor's duties free of charge whenever there was a service at the university church, but obviously his services were not unselfish. On April 3, 1723, almost at the same time as Bach was elected Cantor at St. Thomas's, the university authorities appointed Görner musical director of the university, as he had requested. But according to Bach, not rightly so. Clearly, this was an attempt to place the music of the church services at university outside the authority of the Cantor of St.

Thomas's. So the university at first rejected Bach's request to pay him the 12 gulden his predecessors had received. Four weeks later, he was offered half the sum: six gulden. This seems to have enraged Bach even more, because he then appealed to the Electoral Prince Frederick August I, 'August the Strong.' Probably Bach handed in his letter personally to the court when he was in Dresden in September 1725 to perform two organ concertos. Three days later the university was instructed in a letter from the court of Dresden *to pay the Cantor the required sum to his satisfaction.* The university then started to complain about Bach on several pages to the electoral prince. When Bach was informed of this complaint, he concluded the year 1725 with a 16-page reply plus enclosures which he sent to Dresden on New Year's Eve. August the Strong probably did not read it. Neither did he read the complaint by the university. Whilst we are well-informed about everyday arguments like this during Bach's time in Leipzig through the records of the court of Saxony and national archives, many of his compositions from the same period of his life have been lost. After failing to get the university to agree to his claim, despite the intervention by the court of Dresden, Bach finally gave up all responsibility for music at the university church services. Later, the university and the Cantor of St. Thomas's reached an agreement. Görner remained musical director and also became organist at St. Thomas's in 1729. Bach became director of the students' musical college, which had been founded by Telemann, and which from then on was called 'Bach's musical college.'

In Leipzig the shortage of finance and personnel that Bach had at his disposal for his *ultimate aim of a regulated church music* bothered him most. On August 23, 1730, he wrote a petition to the city council. The head-line read: *Brief, but very necessary Sketch of a Well-Appointed Church Music, and some Impartial Reflections upon the Decay of this Music.* He analyzed the conditions, inveighed against the deplorable state of affairs and made proposals as to how this situation could be improved. He compared the poor payment of the musicians in Leipzig with the generous income of the musicians at the court in Dresden. Indirectly, he accused the council of meanness. Even the length of this *'Brief Sketch'* – it ran to ten pages – indicates a certain agitation. Bach gave vent to his discontentment with the fact that his musical work was constantly hindered by insufficient means. In the city hall of Leipzig, however, there was no Prince Leopold *who loved music and appreciated the arts*, nor was there an August the Strong to spend freely on his artists and their work. Bach's petition came into the hands of thrifty, proud burghers whose concern focused on daily life in the city. They were faithful Christians and knew that one had to go to church, and pray, sing and make music there. But in their opinion, the Cantor of St. Thomas's went too far with his requests. They felt attacked and hurt. They did not answer Bach. In the following two years, the Leipzig city council ignored the Cantor of St. Thomas's whenever allowances or endowments were shared out, and consequently Bach wanted to leave Leipzig. He wrote to Erdmann:

By God's will, I am still here. But since (1) I found out that this post is not as good as I was told before I came here, and (2) many allowances are not being paid, (3) it is a very expensive city and (4) since oddly the authorities here do not appreciate music, and I, thus, have to live with anger, envy and enmities almost all the time, I will be forced to seek a better life elsewhere. If your honour knows of or finds a post which is appropriate for an old, loyal servant here in Leipzig,

87. St. Paul's College, university of Leipzig, in the 18th century. Watercolour.

I humbly ask you to recommend myself.

This request for help was unnecessary. A fortunate coincidence made Johann Matthias Gesner rector of St. Thomas's school at this time. Gesner had admired Bach since his days at Weimar and was a friend of his. He talked the council out of disciplinary action against Bach, and from 1732 on – when he was 47 years old – Bach again received his share of the annual allowances.

In various respects, the year 1730 marked a change in Bach's relationship with Leipzig. He had clearly reached the limits of his post, and his enthusiasm as Cantor for reform seems to have been broken. But fortunately Bach the composer was not affected by this change of attitude. Nobody could hinder him from doing what he pleased on his sheets of music. In day-to-day life Bach remained a realist and a tactician. He did not call the council malicious or unfair, but only *peculiar and not very appreciative of music*. The councillors did not change. The leopard could not change its spots. Bach finally accepted this. Thus, he had to find new arrangements with them. From bitter experience, Bach distrusted the new peace with Leipzig city council. He therefore appealed to the court at

88. Musical instruments of Bach's time.

Dresden and requested the title of court composer. This title would make an impression upon the citizens of Leipzig, and would improve his position in the city. He was right. The last 14 years of his life were lived among the citizens of Leipzig with the title of *Composer of the Royal Court Orchestra* of Dresden. Besides the many cantatas he created *to God's honour*, he praised his earthly patron, the Prince Elector of Saxony and King of Poland, whenever this was necessary. In return, he was supported and sponsored by the court of Dresden. From this point on, the councillors tried to avoid conflict with the Cantor of St. Thomas's and court composer. A man who was protected by the royal court of Dresden, a man highly praised by foreign musical experts – as was the Cantor of St. Thomas's – was respected a little more by the citizens of Leipzig. In this regard, too, they were true burghers.

Bach's Family

The documents and information which have been preserved about Bach's family life paint only a partial picture. Bach's own records are very sparse, even for his time in Leipzig. Besides notes on sheets of paper, he seems not to have written very much. But from the many records which have been preserved in the archives of the city, the university, the parish of St. Thomas's and the court of Dresden, a mosaic can be assembled that shows Bach's personality in the second half of his life.

The most important part of his work, his service in church, will be discussed later, as will Bach's work as a teacher at St. Thomas's school. But even if many records had been written, probably little of excitement apart from the sparse details that are already known about his family life would be discovered. On May 22, 1723, the Bachs moved to the apartment in St. Thomas's school which had been newly renovated for the Cantor. The front of the school bordered St Thomas's churchyard, which had been used formerly as a graveyard and was now surrounded by the school building, the church and six townhouses. From there, narrow alleys led to the market place, the city hall and the district of Pleissenburg. At the back, the schoolhouse and the church of St. Thomas's bordered the western part of the city walls. Through a little gate, known as the 'little door to St. Thomas's', one could cross a moat into the meadows and forests around the city. This must have been a boon for the children, who could play there under the watchful eye of Mrs Bach or of their older brothers and sisters. Johann Sebastian Bach looked out from his 'composing room' via the city wall to the west. The living quarters of the family, however, occupied rooms on three floors of the southern wing of the old building dating from the 16th century. Besides the Cantor, the rector and the alumni, the pupils of the boarding school also lived in the three-storey schoolhouse, which also contained the classrooms. Bach's apartment seems to have been very spacious: there must have been room enough for him and his family, and for the relatives and guests who often lived there temporarily, beside his ever-growing number of children.

From 1723 to 1728, a new Bach child was born each year. Then, after a year without a new child, the next four children followed from 1730 to 1733. Johann Sebastian was 57 years old, and Anna Magdalena 41 when their youngest child was born. The reason why, in most cases, the birth and baptism were recorded under the same date, was the high infant mortality of those years. A new-born child was to be released from original sin as soon as possible by being baptized.

In varied order, daughters and sons were born to the couple. For some, only the dates of their baptism or funeral have been preserved:

Christiana Sophia Henrietta, born and baptized in the spring of 1723 at Cöthen, died July 1, 1726, in Leipzig.
Gottfried Heinrich, born on February 26, 1724, baptized on February 27, 1724,

buried on February 26, 1763, at Naumburg.

Christian Gottlieb, baptized on April 14, 1725, died September 21, 1728, in Leipzig.

Elisabeth Juliana Friederica, baptized on April 5, 1726, died August 24, 1781, in Leipzig.

Ernestus Andreas, baptized on October 30, 1727, died November 1, 1727, in Leipzig.

Regina Johanna, baptized on October 10, 1728, died April 25, 1733, in Leipzig.

Christiana Benedicta, baptized on January 1, 1730, died January 4, 1730, in Leipzig.

Christiana Dorothea, baptized on March 18, 1731, died August 31, 1732, in Leipzig.

Johann Christoph Friedrich, born on June 21, 1732, baptized on June 23, 1732, died January 26, 1795, at Bückeburg.

Johann August Abraham, baptized on November 5, 1733, died November 6, 1733.

Johann Christian, born on September 5, 1735, baptized on September 7, 1735, died January 1, 1782, in London.

Johanna Carolina, baptized on October 30, 1737, died August 18, 1781, in Leipzig.

Regina Susanna, baptized on February 22, 1742, died December 14, 1809, in Leipzig.

Besides the children borne by Anna Magdalena, the children of Bach's first wife lived in the apartment in Leipzig: Catharina Dorothea, born on December 29, 1708; Wilhelm Friedemann, November 22, 1710; Carl Philipp Emanuel, March 8, 1714; Johann Gottfried Bernhard, May 11, 1715 – all of them had been born at Weimar. The first-born daughter, Catharina Dorothea, was 15 when the two coaches arrived in Leipzig with the court Kapellmeister of Cöthen and his family. Bach and his young wife seem to have run their family life frugally; otherwise the harmonious family life which is referred to in surviving documents would hardly be imaginable. As was usual in bigger families, the elder children were supposed to help care for their younger brothers and sisters and educate them – with instructions from their parents. Besides the members of the Bach family, musicians, music editors, instrument-builders, poets, students and pupils frequented the house. The Bachs also had contact with a number of middle-class families from various professions in Leipzig. Carl Philipp Emanuel later wrote that *the house was as busy as a dovecote*. Bach himself received help from his cousin Johann Elias Bach, whom he employed – with a written contract of employment – as private tutor and secretary from 1737 to 1742. This cousin loyally fulfilled any duty and did any job he was given, from writing letters and mailing note material and booklets to purchasing a songbird for Mrs Bach. Thanks to one of his letters, addressed to a Cantor friend in Glaucha near Halle, we have a little insight into Anna Magdalena's living room:

Some years ago I had the special honour of personally meeting your honour in the house of my cousin, Kapellmeister Bach, and now I have the long desired opportunity to write a letter to your honour. When the Kapellmeister recently returned from Halle, he told his dear wife that your honour is in possession of a linnet which can sing very prettily thanks to good training by his teacher; since my cousin's wife is devoted to such birds, I am to ask your honour in this letter if you would sell her this songbird at a good price and send her the bird by safe means.

Carl Philipp Emanuel also reported that his stepmother was very fond of birds and flowers. Besides this cousin, a large number of students also assisted the Cantor of St. Thomas's, especially in the last decade of his life. One of them was Johann Christoph Altnickol, who, as he himself put it, *learned to play the clavier and to write compositions*

89. Carl Philipp Emanuel Bach (1714-1788). Pastel picture, attributed to Gottlieb Friedrich Bach, c. 1733.

with Kapellmeister Bach in Leipzig for several years and had profited so much during these years that he finally became organist at the Wenzelskirche, Naumburg. On January 20, 1749, he married Bach's daughter Elisabeth Juliana Friederica in the church of St. Thomas, Leipzig, and he assisted his aged father-in-law in the last months of his life.

According to the few sources that have been preserved, Bach seems to have been a loving but authoritarian head of his family. When his son Wilhelm Friedemann caused trouble for his father at the age of 28 by incurring debts and leaving home for an entire year, Bach condemned Friedemann's character mercilessly. But at the same time he hoped that, with God's help and with strict fatherly rebukes, he could win him back to the right way. The letters of thanks Johann Elias wrote to his cousin and employer Johann Sebastian prove Bach's friendliness to those who treated him with respect and helpfulness. Again and again Bach helped his colleagues and pupils selflessly when opportunity arose. A strain of sentimentality can also be recognized in the few documents about his private life. He seems to have had a tendency to express his opinion emotionally, sometimes even coarsely. Johann Andreas Silbermann, for example, reported how Bach and his uncle Gottfried tested an organ. Bach had called it *a horse's organ, because you had to work like a horse if you wanted to play this organ.*

That Bach had to take any opportunity to earn money is obvious, considering the number of family members he had to provide for. For this reason, he worked on a thick songbook improving old melodies and composing new hymns, and had his cousin Johann Elias offer his clavier lessons for sale at a bargain price: *So it happens that my cousin will publish some clavier pieces which are excellently composed and will be used predominantly by organists. These will be finished come Easter and will comprise some eighty pages. Your worthy gentleman can purchase a number of the first copies at a good price. Later they will cost much more.*

Bach himself reported in a letter to Georg Erdmann about his family's private music-making: *All of them are born musicians, and I can say that I can perform a complete vocal and instrumental concert with my family, particularly since my present wife sings a good soprano, and my eldest daughter does not sound bad either.* As early as July 1723, Wilhelm Friedemann and Carl Philipp Emanuel began to attend St. Thomas's school. All his life, Bach devoted much care to making his sons good musicians. His labours and his fatherly pride were unusually confirmed by these sons, although there were conflicts between Bach and his genius son, Wilhelm Friedemann. Four of Bach's sons became respected composers themselves, and their works are still played today. These four sons soon made careers, not least due to the reputation of their father, who was respected everywhere for the talents and good training of his students.

Wilhelm Friedemann distinguished himself as an organ improviser of genius and composer of a new kind of clavier sonatas. After attending St. Thomas's school and studying law at the university of Leipzig, he became organist at the Sophia Church in Dresden in 1733, and played the Silbermann organ his father had also often played. As early as his time in Dresden, his undisciplined behaviour caused problems. In 1747, he went to Halle as an organist and musical director, but when he was 54 began to lead the troubled life of a vagabond and alcoholic. His great talent finally broke under his unstable character. Bach saw early the risks that threatened to trouble his son and in vain tried to help him find the right way in life. Wilhelm Friedemann died in

90. Wilhelm Friedemann Bach (1710-1784). Pastel picture, attributed to Gottlieb Friedrich Bach, c. 1733.

1784 in poverty in Berlin.

Carl Philipp Emanuel's life, however, went steadily upwards. After attending St. Thomas's school he studied law at the university of Leipzig and later in Frankfurt-an-der-Oder. Besides his studies, he founded a musical academy in Frankfurt, where among other things he performed his own compositions. In 1738, he went to Berlin, from where he was called to Neuruppin by Crown Prince Frederick of Prussia. When Frederick came to the throne, Carl Philipp Emanuel became chamber musician of the King of Prussia who was later to be known as 'the Great.' He served at the courts of Berlin and Potsdam, and played the harpsichord in Frederick's famous flute concerts, which were recorded for posterity by the painter Adolph Menzel. In 1767, Carl Philipp Emanuel became director of music in Hamburg, where he succeeded his famous godfather Telemann. He was given the honorary title of 'Prussian court Kapellmeister'. Highly paid and highly respected, he died in Hamburg in 1788. Carl Philipp Emanuel was more concerned with his father's musical inheritance than were Johann Sebastian Bach's other sons, and he left posterity many records of Bach's personality, his life and his way of working. Apart from Johann Sebastian's works, Carl Philipp Emanuel's compositions are the most frequently played today of the Bach family.

Johann Christoph Friedrich's career also developed according to his father's wishes and ideas. He too studied law. Bach, who instructed all his sons in music, seems to have been worldly enough to persuade his sons to study law to prepare them better than he had been for their struggles in life. Johann Christoph Friedrich soon turned to music, too. As early as at the age of 17, he was accepted into the court orchestra at Bückeburg, after his father had recommended him in a letter to the Imperial Count of Schaumburg-Lippe. He became concertmaster and director of the court orchestra, and like his brothers composed music and stayed at Bückeburg, where he lived a happy life and was highly respected. He died there in 1795.

The youngest, Johann Christian, had the most brilliant foreign career of all of Bach's sons. He was Bach's favourite son – Johann Sebastian Bach had a special love for his young offspring as have many elderly fathers. After his father's death, the 15-year-old Johann Christian first went to Carl Philipp Emanuel in Berlin who instructed him in music. Four years later he went to Italy. Padre Martini, the leading expert in theory of music in Italy who was to support Mozart a generation later, gave him further instruction in music and helped him make important connections in Italy. Johann Christian became a Roman Catholic and organist at Milan Cathedral. He composed numerous operas in the style of the time, which were performed in Naples, Milan, Paris and other cities. At the age of 24, he became 'Music Master to the Queen of England' in London. As such, he introduced to the English court Kapellmeister Leopold Mozart from Salzburg, with his two highly-gifted children, Wolfgang and Nannerl, made music with the eight-year-old Mozart and instructed him. Mozart composed several works which were motivated by Johann Christian Bach. Even in his opera 'Le nozze di Figaro,' themes by Johann Christian Bach can be detected. This youngest son of Johann Sebastian Bach married a famous Italian singer, the prima donna of the London opera. After a life of success, prosperity and fame that overshadowed any other bearers of the name of Bach for two decades, he is said to have succumbed to alcoholism at the end of his life. He died at the age of 47 in London.

Bach was granted the privilege of seeing his first grandchildren. On December 10, 1745, his first grandchild, son of Carl Philipp

91. Johann Christian Bach as 'Music Master to the Queen of England.' Oil painting by Thomas Gainsborough.

92. Recently-discovered oil painting dating from 1730. It is believed to show Johann Sebastian Bach with three of his sons. The authenticity of the painting has not yet been established.

Emanuel, was christened Johann August in Berlin. Bach himself was godfather to his grandson. Two years later, Anna Carolina Philippina, Carl Philipp Emanuel's second child, was born. She later copied out her grandfather's genealogy, preserving it for posterity. Her godmother was Anna Magdalena.

In 1748, Elisabeth Juliana Friederica Altnickol, Bach's daughter, gave birth to her first son. Godfather to the new-born child, who was christened Johann Sebastian, was his grandfather, Johann Sebastian Bach.

School
and Everyday Life

Even before Bach was elected Cantor of St. Thomas's, some councillors had voiced their concerns as to the capability of the court Kapellmeister of Cöthen – whose musical skill was beyond all doubt – to 'inform' his pupils appropriately. This criticism addressed Bach's weak point. He became an excellent music teacher in the course of the years, and enjoyed this part of his duties at the school of St. Thomas's, passionately committing himself to instructing and supporting talented pupils. But, besides music, he had to teach Latin five lessons a week. He had neither been trained for this job, nor did he feel like doing it. Therefore, he came to an arrangement with a colleague at St. Thomas's school who gave Bach's Latin lessons. The council permitted this. However, Bach had to pay his substitute from his own purse. After Bach's installation on June 1, 1723, the director of the school announced *that the new Cantor would not carry out the teaching at school, but had come to an arrangement with a teacher who would give Bach's Latin lessons and would be paid fifty thalers by the Cantor in return.* This substitution by a colleague, by the name of Carl Friedrich Pezold, soon caused disagreements between Bach and his employers.

At St. Thomas's School there were seven teachers. The Cantor was third in importance after the head and the assistant head, and it was his duty to give three lessons a day, besides his other duties at church. Bach gave lessons in vocal and instrumental music to the senior forms. On Saturday afternoon, the rehearsal for Sunday's cantata took place. Every four weeks, supervision at the boarding school fell to the Cantor. When Bach came to

Leipzig in 1723, St. Thomas's School was very neglected. There were not enough class-rooms, and the few rooms were in a poor state. As a consequence of this situation, wealthy Leipzig citizens increasingly decided against sending their sons to St. Thomas's School, and so its income was reduced. The traditional way of selecting pupils was according to their musical talent for service in church. Under Johann Heinrich Ernesti, who had been rector since 1684 – one year before Bach was born - discipline and order had worsened for many years. The 71-year-old rector had neither the authority nor the strength to improve this situation. The *singing in the alleys and streets* of Leipzig – a profitable affair for both teachers and pupils – ruined their voices. Students of the university also took part in these performances to earn some money.

All these problems affected the Cantor more directly than any other teacher; for the results of his lessons could be assessed by the citizens of Leipzig on Sundays and church festivals. Bach's predecessor, Johann Kuhnau, had appealed repeatedly to the city council to help improve the situation, but in vain. It goes without saying that a musician like Bach was not satisfied with things, and conflicts were only a matter of time. Furthermore, Bach's superior in the church, superintendent Salomon Deyling, was a man who got on quietly with his church job, rather than supporting his new Cantor's wish for reforms. Thus, Bach had to work at the school of St. Thomas's in conditions which were not in the least satisfactory. His post in

93. St. Thomas's School rules, 1723. Title page with a engraving by Johann Gottfried Krüger the Elder.

Leipzig did not come up to his expectations. Presumably Bach appealed to individual councillors to change the situation before he wrote a long petition to the council of the city of Leipzig on August 23, 1730. The councillors must have known about the poor conditions at St. Thomas's School, for they had the school renovated and extended in 1730 and the years following. But since they were dissatisfied with the way Bach handled his duties at school, they seem to have paid no attention to his wishes concerning church music in his first decade in Leipzig. The minutes of the council dated August 2, 1730, indicate the bad atmosphere between the city authorities and the Cantor of St. Thomas's even before Bach's petition concerning the decay of church music enraged the council-

lors. The minutes of the meeting where the councillors originally intended to discuss the condition of the buildings of St. Thomas's School reported:

There have been many discussions about St. Thomas's school; the building needs to be renovated, but further investigations will be necessary. But it has to be considered that the Cantor has been dispensed from giving lessons. Mr Pezold has done his job in an unsatisfactory way. The third and the fourth form urgently need a better teacher. The Cantor was to teach one of the lower forms, but he did not do so appropriately. Besides, he had a pupils' choir leave the city without informing the Mayor beforehand. Furthermore, he had gone on a journey without taking leave, etc. He, therefore, has to be admonished. Now it has to be considered if the classes mentioned above are to be instructed by another person. Mr Kriegel is said to be a good man. This problem has to be resolved.

Royal Counsellor Lange said that everything that had been said about the Cantor was true. He should be admonished and substituted by Mr Kriegel.

Royal Counsellor Steger said: Not only does the Cantor not fulfil his duties, but neither is he willing to answer to the council, nor does he give singing lessons. Some other complaints can be added. A change will be necessary, and a solution to this problem must be found.

Counsellor Born sided with this vote.

Dr Hölzel also sided with this vote.

The Council resolved to reduce the Cantor's payment.

The proposal was unanimously accepted by the nine councillors present. One of them even wanted to have put on record that *the Cantor was incorrigible*. Bach's request concerning the decay of church music (see page 164) only aggravated things in the eyes of the councillors. According to the council's resolution of November 6, 1730, they acted on their dissatisfaction with Bach: when the funds that had been collected in the period without a rector – between Ernesti's death in 1729 and Gesner's taking office in 1730 – were to be shared out, the Cantor was to be ignored. Although the headmaster of St. Thomas's School, Councillor Christian Ludwig Stieglitz, admitted in his proposal for sharing out the funds that the Cantor also worked harder due to the vacancy, only his colleagues received money for their additional work.

Since Bach was no bootlicker, his relationship with the Leipzig council and his work at St. Thomas's School would have become intolerable, if the situation had not radically changed in 1730. Ernesti had been buried on October 24, 1729, with a requiem composed by Bach. One year later, Johann Matthias Gesner became the new rector. Gesner was born in 1691 in Roth, near Nuremberg, and worked at the grammar school at Weimar as a young teacher and co-rector. Since that time he had admired Bach's musical skills. Before being appointed head of St. Thomas's School, he was headmaster of a grammar school at Ansbach in Franconia. He was an experienced teacher and an excellent organizer, and managed to achieve a regulated situation at St. Thomas's School within a short time. During the four years he was headmaster, the school building was renovated and extended, and two new floors added. Instead of the old three-storey house, from 1732 a new five-storey school building stood in St. Thomas's churchyard. This building, very modern at the time, housed St. Thomas's School until it was demolished in 1902. Bach's apartment was also renovated. With Gesner, a new spirit and a supporter of Bach entered St. Thomas's School. He valued the Cantor for his musical genius, not his weak-

94. Inside page of St. Thomas's School rules.

95. Students making music. Engraving, 1727.

nesses as a teacher. Gesner improved the situation between Bach and the council, opening the doors and allowing fresh air into the renovated St. Thomas's School. When he wanted to accept an offer to teach at the university besides working as a rector, the council was stupid enough to object. Hence Gesner left Leipzig and became a professor in Göttingen.

His successor was a man who was later granted the same right, to become professor of theology at the university of Leipzig: Johann August Ernesti, who had been assistant head until then. He was 23 years younger than Bach. After attending the universities at Wittenberg and Leipzig, he had taught in the house of Judge Stieglitz, who was also headmaster at St. Thomas's School. Through Stieglitz's influence, he became assistant head in 1731, when he was only 24. The headmaster and at least of some of the councillors put their confidence in him. In the council's meeting on November 2, 1734, when Johann August Ernesti was elected rector, Stieglitz had put on record *that his office as headmaster at the school of St. Thomas's was made more difficult by the Cantor, because the latter did not do what he had to do at school.* Thus, the new set-up was very unfavourable for Bach if any problems arose between him and the new rector. When Ernesti took up office, Bach composed a cantata in celebration, as was his duty as a Cantor. But compared with the respect he had for Gesner, who was six years younger than he, he had scant respect for Gesner's successor. The two were very different in character. Ernesti was a diplomat, in control of his emotions, smooth in his ways. He spoke with academic precision and unbeatable logic. On the other hand, Bach became more and more long-winded and awkward, and had a tendency for emotional overreaction whenever he felt ignored or not properly

respected. During Gesner's time as rector, Bach had occupied a special rank among the teachers as Cantor, justified because of the importance of his post. Now he was subordinate again. At the beginning, the two different men had no problems; they were even friends, at least officially. Ernesti was godfather to two of Bach's sons. But then the friendly relationship was reduced to alienation and finally bitter enmity. The reason for this was quite trivial. In an oversensitive reaction, Bach made of it a debate on general principles that eventually had to be dealt with by the king. According to school rules, the Cantor selected the prefects, but the rector and the headmaster had to agree to his choice. The prefects were senior pupils who presided over four choir groups, and had to be talented and trained. They had to substitute for the Cantor if he fell ill or was absent for any other reason, but they also had to direct the choir, if the pupils of St. Thomas's had to take part in the services of various churches of the city at the same time. In addition, the prefects had to look after the younger pupils.

The past history of the dispute about the prefect, named Johann Gottlob Krause, is only known because of Ernesti's report, which indicates some inconsequential actions on the part of Bach. After Krause had presided over the other three choirs with Bach's consent, the Cantor considered him totally inappropriate to be prefect of the first choir. The main reason for this seems to have been that the rector had appointed Krause prefect of this choir without discussing the matter with Bach. Bach sent Krause away *with loud shouts and much noise from the choir*, as Ernesti wrote. The rector then confirmed Krause as a prefect and forbade the pupils on threat of punishment to sing under any other prefect. Bach complained to Leipzig city council. Ernesti put his point of

96. Johann Heinrich Ernesti (1652-1729), rector of St. Thomas's School from 1684 to 1729. Engraving by Martin Bernigeroth.

view logically and smoothly, showing the Cantor in an altogether unfavourable light. A certain negligence on the part of Bach in fulfilling his duties at school seems credible; he certainly preferred his musical duties. But in the correspondence between the council, the church board and the two opponents, Ernesti accused Bach of lying and corruption. Since neither the council nor the church board made any real attempt to support the Cantor, Bach finally appealed to the king:

Your Eminence, Great and Mighty King and Electoral Prince, my Lord,
All my life I will be obliged to you for having given me the honour of appointing me court composer for Your Majesty. I am very thank-

128

ful for the protection Your Majesty most generously has granted to me, and, therefore, I now have the courage to ask for your help in my present troubles. According to the school rules, my predecessors, the Cantors of St. Thomas's School in Leipzig always had the right to appoint the prefects for the pupils' choirs, for the simple reason that they knew best which pupil was most suited for this task. I also had acted according to this rule, without anybody's interference. However, the present rector, Mr Johann August Ernesti, claimed for himself the right to appoint a prefect without asking for my approval; to make things worse, he appointed a pupil who is very bad at music. And when I realized this problem and saw myself forced to do something about it because of the disorder in music caused by this appointment and wanted to appoint a pupil who is more capable, the rector, Ernesti, not only strictly opposed my actions, but offended and greatly hurt me by forbidding all the pupils from taking part in any of my performances, on threat of punishment.

This tiresome argument between the Cantor and the rector of St. Thomas's went on for two years. At Easter 1738, Frederick August II and his spouse, Maria Josepha, visited Leipzig. After this visit, for which Bach had composed a festive serenade, the official arguments came to a sudden stop, presumably because of an order from the king. The brilliant cantatas with which Bach praised his king and continued to serve him, raised the composer on a pedestal from which he could endure the quarrels of everyday life in Leipzig in the last decade of his life. Because of the king's influence, Bach seems finally to have received the *satisfaction* he had fruitlessly asked for from the rector and his employers in Leipzig. Officially, there was peace between Ernesti and Bach. But the enmity continued. It affected Bach's work as a teacher at St.

Thomas's school for the rest of his life. From this time on, the teachers and the pupils sided with either the rector or the Cantor, according to their personal and musical sympathies. Pupils at St. Thomas's who wanted to become musicians were called *beer fiddlers* by the rector.

In his professional life, Bach was very pugnacious. Traits of obstinacy, even opinionatedness, cannot be denied. Bach found peace in his faith that gave him the energy for his main task, a *well-regulated church music*. And he found peace in his big family which nevertheless left him enough energy to pursue his professional quarrels. Nobody interfered with Bach's artistic work – and nobody attacked him – with impunity. Like every genius, he had strong views as to whether his behaviour was right or wrong. His impatience with his contemporaries can be seen further in his public dispute with Joseph Adolph Scheibe, a well-known musician and musical writer, an argument that continued for ten years. Between the lines of many printed pages attacking and defending Bach's art, some of his contemporaries showed a measure of understanding of the independence of Bach's compositions. This is also true of some articles praising Bach's genius. Scheibe edited a magazine entitled *'Der Critische Musicus'*, published in Hamburg and read by many musicians in Germany, not least because there were few publications like it. In the sixth issue of this periodical, May 14, 1737, we read:

Mr = = is finally in = = the most excellent of musicians. He is an extraordinary artist on the piano and on the organ, and he met only one man who could compete with him. I heard this great man play several times. His perfect craftsmanship is astonishing, and it is hardly believable how he can cross his fingers and his feet so peculiarly and quickly, how he can expand them and jump over the keys without producing even a single note that does not fit and without contorting his body by these movements. This great man would be admired by entire nations, if he had a more pleasant character and if he did not rob his musical pieces of everything natural through a pompous and confused form and if he did not obscure its beauty by using too much art. Because he takes his own fingers as a yardstick, his pieces are very difficult to play, for he demands the singers and instrumentalists do with their voices and their instruments as he himself does on the clavier. But this is impossible. Any little decorations and any matters of style he spells out with precise instructions; this, however, not only robs his pieces of the beauty of harmony, but also makes the singing very difficult to listen to. All the voices sound together and with equal weight, and you cannot hear the melody. To cut a long story short: He is in music just like Mr von Lohenstein was in poetry. Pompousness led both from the natural to the artificial, from the sublime to the obscure; and both are admired for their hard work and their efforts which were in vain since they are both contrary to nature.

The writer of this letter is anonymous. Allegedly, Scheibe received this article in the form of a letter from a friend. Not until ten years later did he admit to being the author of the article. The name of the composer who is criticized is not mentioned, but every reader knew who was meant by *Mr =*. Bach seems to have been deeply hurt. Which offended him more – the comparison with Daniel Caspar von Lohenstein, who was denounced as a typical representative of pompous poetry of Johann Christoph Gottsched, the prominent Leipzig poet, and by his students, or being referred to as a *musician* – is difficult to say. Probably the latter, if we look at his defence.

Johann Abraham Birnbaum, author and teacher of rhetoric in Leipzig, an eloquent student, and admirer and friend of Bach, came to the composer's defence. His argument ran to many pages and was entitled *'Impartial Comments on a Questionable Item in the Sixth Issue of Der Critische Musicus.'* In his letter he questioned Scheibe's competence and angrily defended the *Court Composer and Kapellmeister of the King of Poland and Electoral Prince of Saxony, Mr Johann Sebastian Bach* against what he thought of as the derogatory description of him as a *musician.* He praised Bach's skill and referred to *the witness of some impartial experts on music who had also been lucky enough to hear this great man on their journeys. They had highly praised his skills and affirmed without feigning respect: There is only one Bach in the world, and nobody is like him.*

We do not know if Bach had a hand in writing this letter. In an answer Scheibe wrote in an appendix to *'Der Critische Musicus'* two months later, he stated:

This letter is to be ascribed to Kapellmeister Bach, since it is first of all his affair, or it was written by one of his friends on his request. At least, the court composer distributed it among his friends and acquaintances with much pleasure on January 8 of this year.

Even a year later, Bach's cousin, Johann Elias, sent Birnbaum's text to a Cantor who was a friend of Bach's with the words. *My cousin and Mr Birnbaum desire to send your honour their compliments and the enclosed pamphlet.* With Bach's help and the help of his friends, the pamphlet was distributed among musicians as were Scheibe's accusa-

97. Johann Matthias Gesner (1691-1761), rector of St. Thomas's School from 1730 to 1734. Oil painting by Elias Gottlob Haussmann.

98. St. Thomas's School before its demolition in 1902.

tions. Notes by Gottsched, Mattheson, Walther and Lorenz Mizler who edited his *'Musicalische Bibliothek Oder Gründliche Nachricht nebst unparteyischen Urtheil von Musicalischen Schrifften und Büchern'* (Musical Library Or Thorough News and an Impartial Opinion about Musical Writings and Books) in Leipzig show how far this controversy had occupied the minds of musicians all over Germany. The criticism by his contemporaries obviously hurt Bach deeply. This public affair also had its positive side-effect: everyone was talking about Bach, at least every music enthusiast. After five years of printing, quoting and editing many arguments, Scheibe summarized: *After four or five years, the parties have reached a truce.*

Bach's party seems to have been the stronger. Scheibe finally tried his hand at satire. In it, he gave a malicious caricature of Bach, who allegedly lived a conceited life high above the heads of his contemporaries as a famous landmark and an untouchable institution. The intellectual controversies of Scheibe show the beginning of a new era with a new concept of art which Bach never understood: The Enlightenment.

'My dear Mr Critical Musician . . .' Scheibe started the alleged letter from a correspondent dated from April 2, 1739, to his magazine.

. . . I am one of the musicians who tried with all their efforts to attain special skill in playing an instrument and in achieving an admirable craftsmanship in composing very artificial things. I could prove not only by quoting all the inhabitants of this city that has the honour of having myself within its walls but also by quoting all the directors of the orchestras of all the surrounding villages that I am the greatest artist in all the world and that I can compose an artificial and peculiar music that confuses all its listeners. Everything goes upside down. Everything is so confusingly worked out that one cannot discern one voice or the other, and never does one recognize the main melody or understand the words. I also oppose anyone who dares criticize my skilfulness or doubt my achievements or refuses to give me the honour of acknowledging that I am the greatest musician and the greatest composer in the world! Of course, if I had lived at the time of the old Greeks (whom I first came to know in your pages, dear sir), I would be remembered with more praise and honour than any wise men or musicians of all times. So, you know who I am and who it is you have to deal with. But now I must explain to you why I write this letter to you. I never had to do with scholarly things. Neither did I read any musical writings or books. I would never have heard of your magazines, if my brother-in-law, the town clerk, had not made me have a look at them. I always thought a musician had only to deal with his art and need not waste his time reading books and dealing with scholarly and philosophical papers.

99. The west side of St. Thomas's School after the renovation of 1732. Coloured engraving.

The funny words and the nonchalant arrogance with which Scheibe alluded to Bach's lack of academic education display one of the worst misunderstandings of modern times: that art and music need a highly educated intellect. Bach's work proves that this is not true. The lack of education and Bach's weaknesses in his everyday life – there may have been many others we do not know about – were no contradiction to his greatness as a composer. Albert Schweitzer compared this greatness to the elemental force of nature:

He accepted the recognition of the world for a master at the organ and the clavier as something natural. But only the contemporary parts of his art were acknowledged. He never asked the world to acknowledge the untimely things of his creation when he uttered the things that lived in his soul. It did not even cross his mind that he could expect such a thing . . . He was the first who did not see the untimely value of his works. In this, he may rank highest among all creative spirits; his unlimited power was confirmed with-

133

out realizing it, like the powers that are active in nature. Therefore, it is as elemental and rich as nature.

It is one of the most astonishing phenomena of the history of civilization that intelligent men like Joseph Adolph Scheibe were blind to elemental forces such as Bach. Scheibe was 27 when he started his attacks against Bach, and 37 when he made his final move: in the preface to the new edition of his *Critische Musicus*, published in 1745, he apologized. *It easily happens in arguments that audacious words say much more than one wanted them to say.* Of course, he continued attacking Bach's passionate defenders.

Two opposing currents in the history of music met. The controversy increased until Bach's death. Young musicians started to turn away from the musical ideal of baroque. They looked for new forms and tones. Scheibe preached the return to 'simple forms.' He admired Gluck. Some of Scheibe's musical theories can even be found in operas of the 19th century. Bach's works, however, contained nothing 'progressive' as the worshippers of anything new would say today. Scheibe did not understand that timeless music cannot be only progressive – as so many critics like him have not understood. For his younger critics, Bach was a living memorial. As early as 1728, when he was 43, the poet Gottsched praised him, feeling that Bach would be celebrated in the future:

Telemann . . . This famous man is one of the three masters of music who bring honour to our country. Handel is admired by all experts in London, and Kapellmeister Bach stands out among his contemporaries in Saxony. They spread their music not only in Germany, but also in Italy, France and England they are well known and loved.

The young people of Bach's time also rebelled against the success and dignity of their fathers, although they did so with the self-control expected of younger generations at the time. Thus, lines of development in the history of music, even in the history of civilization, were drawn where only a disturbance seems to have been caused in Bach's daily life.

100. Johann August Ernesti (1707-1781), rector of St. Thomas's School from 1734 to 1759. Oil painting by Anton Graff.

Bach and the Kings

As early as his service as a young man at Weimar – a dukedom ruled in an absolutist way – Bach had learned how to deal with dukes and court officials. He showed them all the courtesy and respect expected of a loyal subject, whilst always holding his head high. Two generations later, Beethoven made the famous remark: *Nobility can easily be handled, if one has something that makes an impression on them.* That is what Bach knew instinctively. He had his music, and he knew how to use it for his advantage. The revolutionary rebellion against the power of the country's rulers, which was almost natural for many artists a century later, was something Bach never did or wanted to do. Neither did he have any reason to rebel. He did not suffer from arbitrary acts by aristocrats. Rather he had the privilege of enjoying their favour. No single comment by Bach against the kings or princes of his time survives; but there is no evidence that he might have believed in the doctrine of the divine right of kings, as did many of his contemporaries. He was too much of a Lutheran Christian to believe such a doctrine. Just as there were princes of music – he himself became one in his old age – there were political princes. He knew from his own experience that most of the princes were more appreciative of art than the councillors and consistory members of his time. Thus, Bach continued to be a friend of princes, but never did he become their slave. At Cöthen, he had lived in one of the numerous provincial capitals that existed in Germany at that time. The city of Leipzig, however, was part of the electoral principality of Saxony. The Prince Elector of Saxony was one of the most powerful monarchs of Europe. Since 1697 he had also been the ruler of one of the most important regions for agricultural produce and raw materials of Eastern Europe: Poland. August the Strong was called Frederick August I as electoral prince of Saxony, but August II as king of Poland, and his son was called Frederick August II and August III. The young Electoral Prince August I came to power in Poland by an act that was spectacular – and condemned by many of his countrymen: at Baden, near Vienna, he abandoned the Protestant Lutheran faith of his fathers, who had ruled this central Reformation state, and embraced Roman Catholicism. Whenever his name is mentioned, posterity, which has added several hundreds of children to the hundred or so children he did father by numerous women, first of all think of the baroque prince who loved dissipated, luxurious festivities and made Dresden the centre of baroque architecture and encouraged artists to develop their abilities to the full at his court. The monument representing him on the Fortress of Dresden as sort of a Saxon Hercules under the heavy load of the globe has often been ignored. Had he not succeeded in achieving the near-impossible by uniting the two different countries under his power, forming various coalitions with the great powers of Europe for three decades and

101. Frederick August I, called 'August the Strong,' Electoral Prince of Saxony (and August II, King of Poland, 1670-1733). Oil painting by Louis de Silvestre, 1718.

136

102. Dresden, from the right bank of the river Elbe. Oil painting by Bernardo Bellotto, called Canaletto II, 1748.

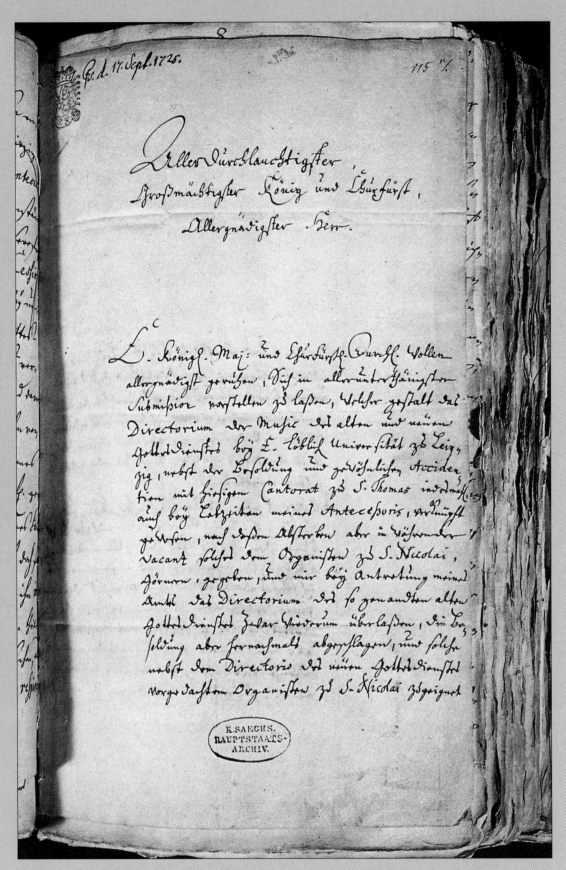

103. Petition by Bach on September 14, 1725, to Electoral Prince Frederick August I of Saxony.

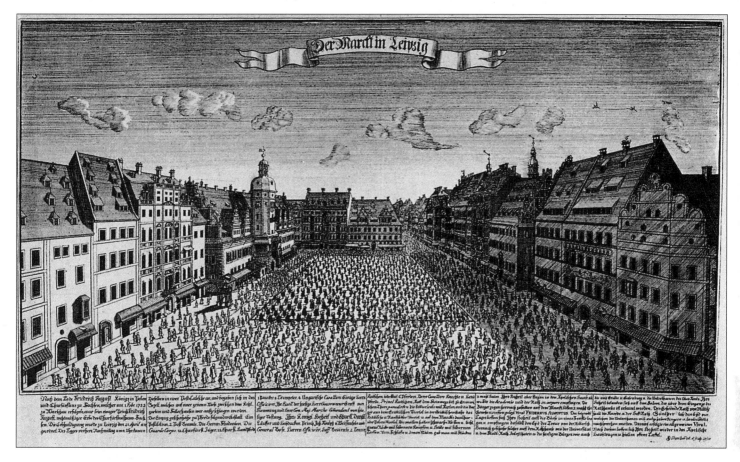

104. The homage in the market-place of Leipzig on April 21, 1733 on the occasion of the enthronement of Frederick August II. Engraving by Johann Christoph Sysang.

bringing them economic prosperity, Dresden could not have become a centre of European culture in the 18th century. With laws, edicts and many clever personal moves, he supported industry, trade, architecture and science in both countries, thus creating the economic preconditions for the brilliant peak of the baroque age in Saxony which posterity has rightly called 'Augustan.'

The country where the evangelical Lutheran Cantor of St. Thomas's in Leipzig lived and worked was ruled by one of the most important Roman Catholic kings of Europe. From his guest recitals as an organ virtuoso, Bach was already known at the court of Dresden when he moved from Cöthen to Leipzig. We do not know when he was first introduced personally to August. Bach's letter, dated September 14, 1725, in

which he asked for the king's intervention at the university of Leipzig, as well as subsequent letters to the king, indicate that the king was acquainted with Bach. In spite of that, Bach had only a few contacts with the court of Dresden during his first ten years in Leipzig. Composing and performing cantatas praising the king and his family did not form part of Bach's duties as Cantor. On appropriate occasions, secular works of this kind could be performed before the king to whom they had been dedicated. When August the Strong came to Leipzig in May 1727, his birthday on May 12 was such an occasion. At a great celebration like that which was to take place at the market-place of Leipzig, *everything had been prepared for making music, which was then performed to the King's satisfaction and in front of a big crowd of people who were held back by soldiers who protected His Majesty from the crowd*. This was recorded in Christoph Ernst Sicul's 'Annals of Leipzig' dating from the year 1727. Only the libretto by Christian Friedrich Haupt has been preserved of the celebratory cantata by Bach, *'Entfernet euch, ihr heitern Sterne'* (Go away, you happy stars). A few months later, when August the Strong celebrated his saint's day, on August 3, 1727, Bach dedicated another cantata to the king: *'Ihr Häuser des Himmels, ihr scheinenden Lichter'* (O houses of the sky, O shining lights). This cantata too has been lost, except for a few sheets of music. Only the libretto by Christian Friedrich Henrici, who wrote under the pseudonym of Picander, and whom we will meet as librettist of many cantatas Bach composed in Leipzig, has been preserved in its entirety. The same is true of a third secular cantata Bach composed five years later, in 1732, for August's saint's day: *'Es lebe der König, der Vater im Lande'* (Long live the king, the father in our country).

August's wife, Electoral Princess Christiane Eberhardine, was highly esteemed by Saxony's Protestant population because of her loyalty to her Lutheran faith. She refused to join her husband in becoming a Roman Catholic. After living a quiet life at the castle of Pretsch on the Elbe, she died on September 5, 1727. A well-to-do Leipzig student, Carl von Kirchbach, took the initiative for a memorial service at the university church. He commissioned the libretto for a mourning ode from Gottsched and music from Bach. After some disagreements with the authorities of the university (who wanted to have the ode composed by their musical director, Görner, and not by Bach), Bach's cantata, *'Laß, Fürstin, laß noch einen Strahl'* (Let, O Princess, let one more light; BWV 198) was performed under his direction at the memorial service. A procession of representa-

tives of the council and university moved from the main city church, St. Nikolai's, to St. Paul's, *while all the bells were ringing*, as a Leipzig annual recorded. The report reminds us of the fourth recitative in Bach's funeral music: *The ringing sound of the bells*.

August the Strong died in Warsaw on February 1, 1733, at the age of 63. His 37-year-old son, Frederick August II (and as king of Poland August III) succeeded to the throne. He had been married to Maria Josepha, née archduchess of Austria, in 1719. The new electoral prince and king became one of Bach's most important supporters, and the composer dedicated many compositions to the monarch. Bach may have been introduced to him personally as early as September 1731, when Bach was at the court of Dresden to give concerts. A few months after Frederick August II came to power, Bach dedicated the first cantata to the new ruler on the occasion of his saint's day: *'Frohes Volk, vergnügte Sachsen'* (Happy nation, joyful Saxons). Again only Picander's libretto has been preserved. It was to be followed by a number of other cantatas in the years to come. Festive occasions such as the saint's day or birthday of his king, the electoral prince, the queen, the coronation, the anniversary of their enthronement or the royal couple's visit to Leipzig were occasions for Bach to compose his secular cantatas. Some titles such as *'Tönet, ihr Pauken! Erschallet, Trompeten'* (Sound, O timpani! Sound, O trumpets; BWV 214) or *'Auf, schmetternde Töne der muntern Trompeten'* (Let yourselves be heard, loud tones of the happy trumpets; BWV 207a) indicate the brilliant instruments he used to make his cantatas sound festive. In this music, and in that

105. Frederick August II, Electoral Prince of Saxony (and August III, King of Poland) (1696-1763). Oil painting by Louis de Silvestre, 1736.

of Georg Frideric Handel, Baroque pomp reached its secular peak. They were fascinating sounds for the monarchs praised in them. Thanks to Bach's art, these works composed for a specific purpose have become timeless treasures. These works brought not only esteem and the king's good will, but also a good income to the composer. For example, Bach signed a receipt for the cantata *'Willkommen, ihr herrschenden Götter der Erden'* (Welcome, you ruling gods on earth) of which only Gottsched's libretto has been preserved: *Fifty-eight thalers for the evening serenade performed for His Majesty and others on April 27, 1738.* In an enclosure to the receipt, he shared out the royal fees: *Fifty thalers for myself, and eight thalers for the Stadtpfeifers.*

Most of these secular compositions came into being during his second decade in Leipzig. In the first years, the newly appointed Cantor of St. Thomas's devoted himself almost entirely to his duties in church music. Around 1730, the composition of secular works increased. In only a few years, Bach had composed a great number of church cantatas that were, together with the works he had composed at Weimar, basic materials for the ecclesiastical year and could be used in further recitals. His passions had also been finished at that time. From 1729 on, he needed secular compositions for the musical college. His experiences with the council, the school and church authorities had robbed Bach of his initial enthusiasm for his duties in Leipzig. All these circumstances increased his interest in Dresden. He became friends with the famous Kapellmeister of the court opera, Johann Adolf Hasse, and his wife, a well-known singer. Dresden was considered the centre of contemporary Italian music in Germany. The court music in Dresden gave Bach some useful ideas for his own compositions. Last but not least, Bach seems to have liked Frederick August II and his wife Maria Josepha, with their relatively modest lifestyle, more than the audacious, powerful August the Strong, whose dissipated private life had been notorious.

On April 21, 1733, the new royal couple came to Leipzig to present themselves to the city's government, to the church and the inhabitants and to be feted. At the homage service at St. Nikolai's, Bach's B minor Mass (BWV 232) was performed for the first time. When Bach asked the king three months later for the title of Court Composer, he enclosed with his letter the manuscript of the Kyrie and the Gloria in his own handwriting, and in that of Anna Magdalena, Wilhelm Friedemann and Carl Philipp Emanuel. The date of this petition to the court of Dresden indicates that Bach personally handed in the documents at court.

Your Most High Electoral Prince,
Your Most Generous Majesty,
I most humbly submit to Your Majesty this modest work of the science of music of which I am a devoted servant, most humbly begging you not to judge it by its poor composition but according to your mercy which is known all over the world, and to place me under your protection. For some years I have been director of music of the two main churches of Leipzig, but I have had to endure some offences and sometimes even a shortfall in the allowances for my work through no fault of my own. These offences would come to an immediate stop, if Your Majesty gave me the honour of bestowing upon me the title of a court composer and issued a decree to the respective authorities. If Your Majesty grants

106. Frederick August II's wife, Maria Josepha, Electoral Princess of Saxony and queen of Poland, née archduchess of Austria (1699-1757). Oil painting by Louis de Silvestre, 1737.

my humble request, I will be obliged to praise you forever, and I offer my services in humbly obeying your orders any time Your Royal Majesty gives me the honour of asking for a composition of church music or for the orchestra, and I will always loyally be obliged to committing my energies to your service.

To Your Royal Majesty
Dresden
July 27
1733.

Your most humble
and obedient servant,
Johann Sebastian Bach.

But the king had to defend the enormous economic, cultural and political inheritance from his father – which was very important in European power politics – against controversies at home and enemies abroad, and at the beginning of his reign was concerned with other things than with appointing Bach court composer. The war in Poland forced him to remain away from Dresden for two years. At last, after the king's return and a second petition by Bach, Frederick August II did as Bach wished on November 19, 1736:

Accordingly Your Majesty, the King of Poland and Electoral Prince of Saxony etc. gives himself the honour of bestowing upon Johann Sebastian Bach the title of a composer for the court orchestra as the latter had most humbly asked for and because of his excellent skilfulness. A decree of appointment has been issued, signed with the signature of Your Royal Majesty and affixed with the royal seal.

Under August the Strong German civilization, sciences and arts reached an unprecedented peak in Dresden and Saxony, but one cannot fail to notice that music played a minor role compared to the other arts. The great personalities of Augustan baroque were the architect Matthäus Daniel Pöppelmann, the sculptor Balthasar Permoser, the goldsmith Johann Melchior Dinglinger and their many assistants; but there was no musician at the court of Dresden of comparable importance. This is even more astonishing if one considers that the musicians at the court of Dresden had an income and a social prestige that was unheard of in any other royal capital of Europe at the time. August the Strong, who liked to be surrounded by artists and artistic influences from all over the world, who encouraged his artists to create works of unique beauty and technical perfection, who advised them and who directed them without regimenting them, obviously had little feeling for music. Otherwise he would have acknowledged Johann Sebastian Bach and his work as much as he acknowledged the other arts. His son and successor, Frederick August II, was unimportant by comparison. He too was a passionate supporter of the arts, and seems to have had a deeper sense of music, but even for him, the only purpose of music was to decorate social events. Besides, for long periods of his life, he was concerned with defending his father's legacy by military and political means, and later with coping with the collapse of this inheritance; with his limited resources he was unable to commit himself to supporting the arts in the same way as his brilliant father. Thus, Bach never had a close relationship with the Dresden court. It was more or less limited to his petition for the king's favour and the distant protection the court granted him. He was protected rather than supported by the court. Even if it was not very impressive, this relationship was the only glorious chapter which the Augustan baroque period added to the history of music.

Bach's most important task was, and continued to be, *well-regulated church music*. He never lost sight of this aim when he approached the Dresden court. The title of

107. Autograph MS of the B minor Mass (BWV 232).

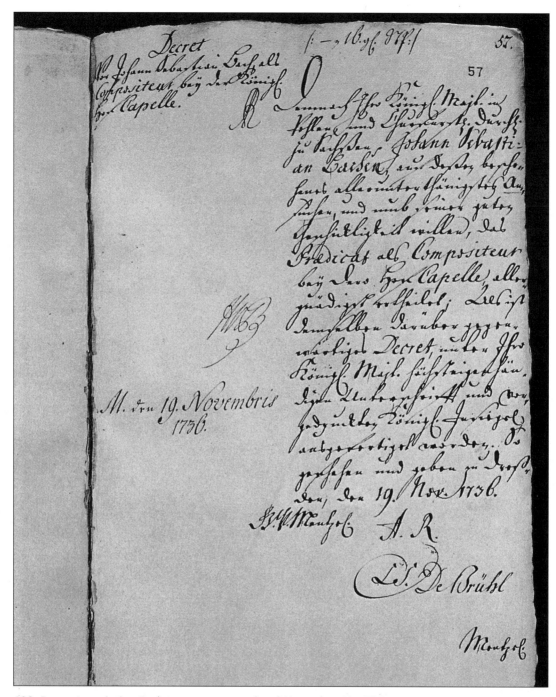

108. Decree appointing Bach court composer, dated November 19, 1736.

Saxon court composer finally also helped him do his work in Leipzig with less interference. In the eyes of the electoral princes of Saxony, Bach remained the Cantor of St. Thomas's in Leipzig who now and then also demonstrated his *excellent skilfulness* as the decree appointing him court composer said.

At the end of his life, in May 1747, the 62-year-old Bach even met the King of Prussia. Two years earlier, in 1745, Frederick II (later called 'Frederick the Great') had defeated the Saxon troops in the Second Silesian War in battles near Striegau and Kesselsdorf and forced the Saxons to sign the humiliating Peace of Dresden. Ten years later he forced Electoral Prince Frederick August II to flee to

109. The palace of Sanssouci.

Poland and thus put to an end the Saxon-Polish dynasty. Frederick II of Prussia was 35 when he received Bach at Potsdam. The young king was considered the musician and poet among the rulers of Europe of the time. After a tough time as a young man under the influence of the military style of his father, the 'warrior-king' Frederick William I, Frederick II had come to power in 1740. In the same year, he appealed to all foreign artists to come to Prussia. Many came, although they may not have been the most prominent artists of Europe of the time. From 1744 on, Frederick II had Potsdam castle renovated, intending to stay there in winter. One year later, the works at the new summer palace of Sanssouci began. According to Frederick's wishes and intentions, Georg Wenzeslaus von Knobelsdorff, who had been appointed director of the Prussian building and construction project by the king, directed the renovation of the palace at Potsdam, which had been an occasional lodging place until then, and made it the new centre of art in Prussia. This palace was to leave its mark on European culture and its style was to be referred to as 'Frederician Rococo.' *Sparta changed and became Athens*, Voltaire commented with his French sense of humour, when he visited Potsdam in 1743. Thanks to Frederick the Great, Potsdam became the centre of Prussia. His predecessors had only stayed there now and again, but he made it his permanent royal capital and lived there until his death. Only in times of war, or when unavoidable duties made it necessary, did he stay in nearby Berlin, the Prussian capital. Voltaire, who spent his famous three years at Potsdam from 1750 to 1753 as Frederick's guest, had many interesting talks with him on philosophical themes. As he scoffed: *There is a surprising number of bayonets, but only a few books to be found*. But Frederick the Great had taken his father's club, where the Prussian notables had sat on hard wooden chairs drinking beer and cracking jokes, and made of it a place where artists and craftsmen, philosophers and musicians could develop their abilities to the full during his rule. In the beautiful gardens which still surround the castles in Potsdam today, the Prussian dream of supremacy died away.

Bach came to this new centre of art when he arrived at Potsdam on May 7, 1747, together with his eldest son, Wilhelm Friedemann. Bach's reasons for coming must have been both to see his son Carl Philipp Emanuel, his daughter-in-law and his grandchild, and the prospect of meeting the Prussian king. In the last years of his life, Bach hardly left Leipzig. The '*Berlinischen Nachrichten*' reported the official part of this visit:

From Potsdam it has been reported that last Sunday the famous Kapellmeister from Leipzig, Mr Bach, arrived with the intention of enjoying listening to the excellent music at court. In the evening, when the chamber music in the royal apartments usually begins, His Majesty was informed that Kapellmeister Bach was in Potsdam and was waiting in the anteroom for the most generous permission of the King to be allowed to listen to the music. The King immediately ordered that he be asked to enter. When Bach entered into the room, the King went to the pianoforte and without preparation started to play a theme. Then he asked the Kapellmeister to play a fugue to this theme. The Kapellmeister did so in such a brilliant way that His Majesty showed his pleasure at it, and all those present were highly astonished. Mr Bach liked the theme

110. Frederick II, King of Prussia, called 'Frederick the Great' (1712-1786). Oil painting by Anna Dorothea Therbusch after Antoine Pesne, c. 1750.

so much that he intends to write it down in a fugue and have it printed in a copperplate. On Monday, this famous man could be listened to on the organ of the Church of the Holy Spirit in Potsdam, where he received much applause from the many listeners who had gathered. In the evening, His Majesty once again asked him to play a fugue with six voices which he did just as skilfully as he had done before, to the King's great pleasure and general surprise.

The same report could be read in newspapers in Hamburg and in Magdeburg. Bach's first biographer, Johann Nikolaus Forkel, who lived from 1749 to 1818 and could interview Bach's sons and many of his contemporaries for his record of Bach's life, reported that this encounter took place at Frederick's request. Since the king constantly made music with Carl Philipp Emanuel, Bach's son is supposed to have initiated this meeting, whoever may have been the first to ask for this encounter – the King of Prussia or the King of Music, as Frederick II is said to have referred to Bach. These meetings are supposed to have taken place at the palace at Potsdam where the king held his chamber music evenings from 7 to 9pm every evening. But, if the evenings of May 1747 were warm, it is equally possible that the scene of this encounter was the summer palace of Sanssouci, which had been ceremonially opened one week before Bach's visit. The report in the newspapers corresponded more or less with the dedication Bach wrote in the preface of the first edition of his late work '*Musikalisches Opfer*' (Musical Offering; BWV 1079). This composition was his way of showing his gratitude to the King of Prussia for his friendly reception two months earlier:

I hereby most humbly dedicate to Your Majesty a Musical Offering whose most brilliant part comes from Your Majesty's own hands. With respectful joy, I remember the grace with which the King played a theme to a fugue on the clavier when I was in Potsdam and then in his grace asked me to play a fugue in His Majesty's presence. Of course, I was obliged to do as Your Majesty wished. But I soon detected that, due to a lack of preparation, the recital was not as good as such a brilliant theme demanded. Therefore, I decided to work out this royal theme and then make it known to the world, which I immediately started to do.

111. The grand piano of Frederick the Great, an instrument built by Gottfried Silbermann.

Bach's Service in the Church

We understand a Cantor to be an expert in sacred music who fulfils his duties in church. He plays almost exclusively works which have been handed down in the repertoire. Only very rarely does he perform in secular concerts. It is hard to imagine a man like today's Cantor at St. Thomas's in Leipzig being at the same time an expert composer of secular music. In Bach's day it was different: being Cantor did not exclude composing and performing secular music, nor did the post of Kapellmeister exclude the creation of sacred music. The fact that Bach composed both secular and sacred music was nothing unusual in his time. Only the skilfulness with which he fulfilled both tasks made him prominent among the composers of his time. Secular music ranked second for Bach, the faithful Christian and servant of his church.

Today's *Bachwerke-Verzeichnis* (BWV; list of compositions by Bach) involves some problems that have to be discussed briefly. Music enthusiasts read these BWV numbers on the covers of records and CDs and in books. Bach's last composition, the *'Art of the Fugue,'* has the BWV number 1080. It is understandable that many music enthusiasts assume that Bach composed 1080 works. But 188 BWV numbers are assigned to chorales of which Bach had written only the melody. Another 69 numbers are assigned to the so-called *Schemellische Gesangbuch* (Schemelli Hymnbook) which a colleague of Bach's, Cantor Georg Christian Schemelli, had edited in 1736. Of the 69 basso continuo movements it comprises, only two are certainly original compositions by Bach, and there is one that might be composed by him. The second *'Little Clavier Book for Anna Magdalena Bach'* is listed with 11 BWV numbers. But of the songs and arias written in this booklet, only four can be ascribed to Bach with certainty. There are 220 BWV numbers for clavier works, and it has to be taken into consideration that short didactic pieces have their own BWV numbers, as have the famous *'Goldberg Variations'*. In addition, the authenticity of 12 clavier pieces is controversial. Another almost insoluble problem is that again and again Bach inserted entire pieces of former compositions into later works. Thus, an undisputed list and count of his musical legacy is impossible.

Strictly speaking, not more than 800 compositions of various lengths can really be considered original works by Bach. How many of these compositions are sacred and how many secular? To the 245 previously-known organ compositions have been added 33 more pieces recently rediscovered in America. Of course, this total of some 280 organ works cannot be compared with the 200 or so extant church cantatas, for these organ works are all short pieces, whereas each cantata has an average length of 20 minutes; some are even longer. The performance time of the passions, oratorios and masses is several times longer. Even if we ignore the estimated 100 church cantatas that have been lost and the few motets Bach composed, he has left us some 500 sacred compositions, compared with about 300 secular works. If the lengths

112. St. Thomas's church today.

113. St. Thomas's churchyard with St. Thomas's School, renovated after 1732. Coloured engraving by Johann Georg Schreiber.

of the individual pieces are taken into account, sacred works occupy an even higher place. His entire secular output comprises some 200 clavier pieces, 40 cantatas and the same number of chamber music compositions. Of the three dozen secular orchestral works whose composition has been discovered so far, fewer than thirty are still extant. The three dozen preserved transcriptions by Bach comprise both sacred and secular works.

There is no reason to believe that this pro-portion of sacred and secular music came about by accident, that for example more secular compositions than sacred compositions might have been lost. The mere numerical predominance of sacred works indicates how important they were for Bach. With his compositions as Cantor, Bach completely subordinated himself to the liturgy of his church. He never left the geographically limited space of his home in central Germany. Although his church music came into being without any attempt to create interdenominational music,

this music and the deep faith it contains have become a religious treasure for the world and have united people of different denominations in prayer and worship.

The attempts by later generations to interpret his compositions 'spiritually' would have been totally foreign to Bach. He did his everyday work like any other man; probably he was busier doing so than most others, but he never thought of creating works for humanity. Bach had to perform a cantata on every Sunday and holy day of the ecclesiastical year. If the church holy days celebrated in 18th

century Leipzig are added to the Sundays (except for the Sundays during Lent, when no cantatas were performed), Bach had to perform 55–60 cantatas a year. (The exact number depended on the number of holy days that happened to be Sundays.) Cantatas for the services for the annual change of the council, for weddings, funerals and other special occasions were added. In the main service, a cantata usually began after the Gospel had been read. If it had two parts, the second part was played after the end of the sermon or during Communion. Bach himself noted

114. St. Nikolai's church. Engraving by Gabriel Bodenehr the Elder, 1749.

such a liturgy in Leipzig on the back of the title page of his cantata '*Nun komm, der Heiden Heiland*' (Now come, saviour of the heathens; BWV 61):

*Liturgy of the Service in Leipzig
on the 1st Sunday in Advent in the morning*

(1) Prelude. (2) Motet. (3) Prelude to the Kyrie, if sung. (4) Intoning at the altar. (5) Reading of the epistle. (6) Singing of the litany. (7) Prelude to the chorale. (8) Reading of the Gospel. (9) Prelude to the main music. (10) Singing of the creed. (11) The sermon. (12) After the sermon, some verses of a

hymn are sung as usual. (13) The Eucharist. (14) Prelude to the music. And after that, preludes and chorales are sung alternately, until the end of the Communion.

This list also shows how much work an organist had to do during a main service. Although the Cantor was responsible for the cantata, it was not his duty to play the organ himself; each church had its own organist. But Bach certainly substituted for the organist several times; occasionally he may even have ousted them, if the organ recital was particularly important to him for the musical performance of the service. From the 2nd to the 4th Sunday in Advent and during Lent before Easter, no main music was performed at church at all, except for the Annunciation on March 25. Bach's oratorios and passions seem to have been composed during these quiet times of meditation, when the Cantor was free from his weekly duty to compose or revise a cantata, to rehearse it and perform it on Sunday.

As *musical director*, Bach was responsible for the music at the main church of St. Nikolai, at St. Thomas's, at the New Church and at St. Peter's. In the New Church, *nothing but motets and chorales* was sung, as Bach wrote in a petition to the council, and in St. Peter's only chorales were sung. From 1723 to 1725, cantatas for the services on Christmas, Easter, Pentecost and on Reformation Day at St. Paul's, the university church, were part of Bach's duties. From 1726 on, Bach left this work to Görner, after long discussions and tedious attempts to make it part of his own duties. Obviously, the weight of his duties was too much for him. The cantatas were performed alternately at St. Nikolai's and at St. Thomas's every other week. Although St. Thomas's school had to provide the four churches with choirs, and St. Thomas's was the real centre of church music in Leipzig for this reason, at St.

Nikolai's, special festival services took place, where Superintendent Deyling was senior preacher. At St. Nikolai's, the St. John Passion (BWV 245) was performed for the first time on Good Friday 1724. The St. Matthew Passion (BWV 245) was first performed in 1727 at St. Thomas's according to latest research – not in 1729, as had been assumed until recently. Both churches also claim to have hosted the performance of the St. Mark Passion, whose score and vocal parts have been lost. Bach used parts of this Passion (which was first performed in 1731) in various cantatas. At these two churches, the six parts of the Christmas Oratorio (BWV 248) were also first performed. This is documented in a copy of the first edition of the text which was found at the end of the 19th century in the archives of St. Nikolai's church. On twelve pages, the texts of all six cantatas of the oratorio are united. The title reads: *'ORATORIO which was performed at Holy Christmas in both main churches of Leipzig in 1734.'* The Easter Oratorio *'Kommt, eilet und laufet'* (Come, hurry and run, BWV 249) and the Ascension Oratorio *'Lobet Gott in seinen Reichen'* (Praise God in his kingdoms; BWV 11) seem to have been performed at St. Nikolai's and at St. Thomas's for the first time. All these works are performed by fine soloists, choirs and orchestras from many countries on special occasions today, yet they were basically works Bach wrote as part of his daily duties in church. This is something we must never forget.

Bach composed all his cantatas for performance by himself. He had, of course, a restricted number of singers and musicians at his disposal, and the quality of performances was often limited by this. Fortunately for posterity, the quality of his compositions was not affected by these circumstances. He seems to have demanded a lot of his singers and instrumentalists, sometimes perhaps too

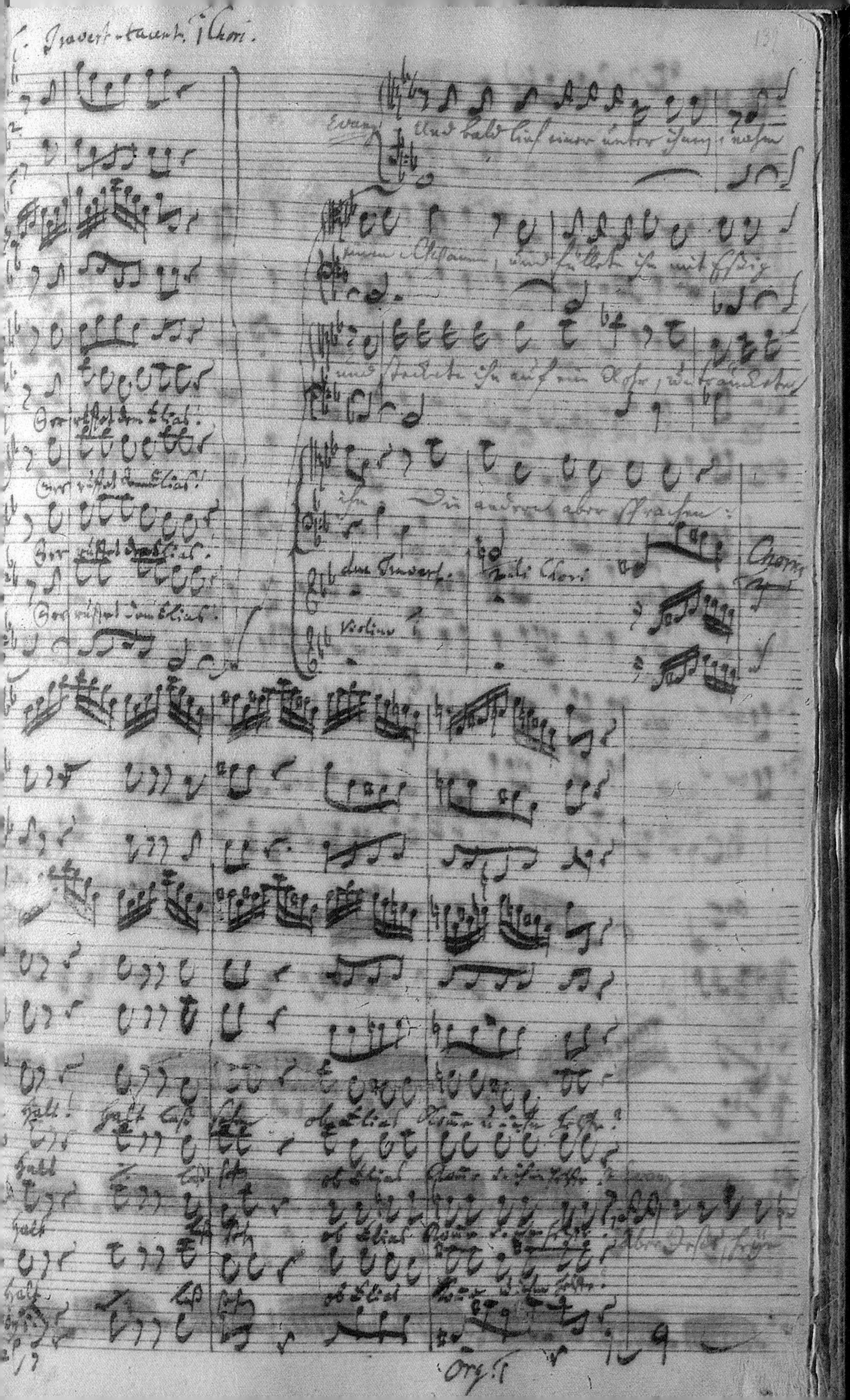
Evang.
Halt!
Org.

much. A document dated May 18, 1729, about splitting up the pupils into the individual choirs, shows how he used the 55 boys of St. Thomas's School for the four choirs: one choir for each of the two main churches, St. Nikolai's and St. Thomas's, and two for the two other churches. Bach's main choirs usually consisted of twelve voices each; three pupils sang treble, alto, tenor and bass. The first singer of each group also had to sing the solo parts. There were no soloists in today's meaning of the word. Professional singers may have entered the dreams of Cantors of Bach's time when they were able to attend an occasional opera performance. Pupils and students were the first to sing the arias and recitatives of the St. Matthew Passion and of all the other compositions by Bach. There may have been compromises. However, the training of voices and the technique of singing had reached a level at that time that has since been lost; likewise the impressive craftsmanship of the builders of the great European cathedrals has been lost.

The Leipzig city council paid eight musicians who worked under the Cantor of St. Thomas's: four Stadtpfeifers, three violinists and an assistant. The senior of these town musicians, the trumpeter Gottfried Reiche, and Bach were personal friends. Bach composed many of his wonderful trumpet arias for him. Reiche's skill seems to have surpassed that of the other musicians. Each of the eight musicians could play several instruments, as was usual at the time, and thus could be employed in many ways. Bach's own description tells us that he had to add 10 to 12 students and pupils to these professional musicians in order to be able to form an orchestra of 18 to 20 members. This ensemble was often reduced by illness, as were the choirs. The orchestra seems to have been augmented sometimes, but this was only done for special festivals. Bach himself directed the musicians and singers from the organ or harpsichord, sometimes even from the violin or viola.

In his memorandum to the city council dated August 23, 1730, Bach described at length the situation he had to cope with in Leipzig church music. When reading this memorandum, we should remember that Bach wrote it to persuade the councillors to spend more money on church music. For this reason, he may have exaggerated slightly in describing the bad situation.

115. Autograph MS of the St. Matthew Passion (BWV 244).

116. Interior of St. Thomas's church before 1885. Goauche by Hubert Kratz.

Brief, but very Necessary Sketch of Church Music and Some Impartial Reflections on the Decay of this Music.

For a well-appointed church music vocalists and instrumentalists are needed.

In this city, the vocalists are pupils of St. Thomas's; there are four groups of them: trebles, altos, tenors and basses.

In order that the sacred choruses may be performed as they should be, the vocalists should be divided up into two groups: the concertists and the ripienists.

Usually there are four concertists, sometimes even five, six, seven or eight, if you want to perform music for two choirs.

There should be eight ripienists as well, two for each voice.

The instrumentalists are also divided up into different groups: as violinists, oboists, flautists, trumpeters and drummers. Let it be noted: Among the violinists, there are also those playing the viola, violoncello and violones.

The number of pupils at St. Thomas's is 55. These 55 are divided up into four choirs for the four churches where they are to play or sing motets and chorales. In the three churches – St. Thomas's, St. Nikolai's and the New Church – the pupils have to be very talented in music. The others go to St. Peter's church – these are those who do not know much about music, but are more or less able to sing a chorale.

Each choir must at least have three trebles, three altos, three tenors and just as many basses, so that at least a two-choir motet can be performed, if one of them falls ill (as happens very often, and particularly at this time of the year, as the prescriptions by the school's doctor for the chemist's shop indicate). (Note: Although it would be even better if the choirs were formed in such a way that each voice has four pupils, and each choir could have 16 members.)

Thus, the number of those trained in music should be 36. Instrumental music should have the following voices:

2 or even 3 for	the 1st violin.
2 or 3 for	the 2nd violin.
2 for	the 1st viola.
2 for	the 2nd viola.
2 for	the violoncello.
1 for	the violone.
2 or, if possible, even 3 for	the oboe.
1 or 2 for	the bass.
3 for	the trumpets.
1 for	the drums.

This makes at least 18 people for instrumental music. N.B. If a piece of sacred music is composed so that flutes are also included (either recorders or traverse flutes), as is done very often, at least two persons are needed as flautists. Thus, we have a total of 20 instrumentalists.

The number of professionals employed to make church music is eight: four Stadtpfeifers, three violinists and one apprentice. Modesty forbids me to speak about their quality and musical skilfulness. However, it has to be considered that some of them are *emeriti*, and the practice of some is not as it should be.

They are divided up as follows:

The 1st trumpet	is played by Mr Reiche
The 2nd trumpet	is played by Mr Genssmar.
The 3rd trumpet	is vacant.
The drums	are vacant.
The 1st violin	is played by Mr Rother.
The 2nd violin	is played by Mr Beyer.
The viola	is vacant.
The violoncello	is vacant.
The violone	is vacant.
The 1st oboe	is played by Mr Gleditsch.
The 2nd oboe	is played by Mr Kornagel.
The 3rd oboe	is vacant.
The bass	is played by the apprentice.

Thus, the following are absolutely needed to reinforce the orchestra and to play the indispensable parts:

2 violinists, for	playing the 1st violin.
2 violinists, for	playing the 2nd violin.
2 people	playing the viola.
2 violoncellists.	
1 violonist.	
2 flautists.	

The missing musicians have had to be substituted partly by students, but in most cases by pupils. The students were willing to do this, in the hope that some of them would be recognized and be given a scholarship or grant (as was the usual practice some time ago). But this did not happen; instead, the few allowances that were spent on the choir before have been successively withdrawn, and the students' willingness has declined, since nobody is willing to work or do a service without being paid accordingly. Besides, it has to be noted that the 2nd violin has mostly, and the viola, violoncello and violone have always, been played by pupils (for lack of better musicians). Thus, it can easily be imagined how the choir has been affected by this situation. This has only affected the music on Sundays. But if I am to speak of the music on holy days (when I have to provide for the music in both main churches at the same time), the shortage of necessary musicians becomes even more apparent, particularly since those pupils who can play one instrument or another have to assist in the other choir, which is the only possible way to have enough instrumentalists.

Speaking of these problems, it has to be mentioned that due to the acceptance of so many boys who have no talent for music, the quality of music has inevitably declined. For it is understandable that a boy who does not know anything of music and who cannot even form a clear tone in his throat cannot be talented in music and consequently can never be used for making music. And there are some who have some basic understanding when they start attending St. Thomas's School, but cannot be employed immediately as they should, because there is not enough time to instruct them before they can be used. Instead of that, they are divided up into the choirs and at least have to be able to keep time and keep in tune to be used at services, as soon as they are received at the school. Besides, every year, some of those who have been instructed in music leave school and are replaced by others, some of whom cannot yet be used; most of these will never be able to make music. Thus, it can easily be seen that the choir deteriorates.

It is well known that my predecessors in the Cantorate, Mr Schell and Mr Kuhnau, needed to ask for the assistance of some students to be able to perform complete and pleasant music. They seem to have been successful, since some of the vocalists, the bass and the tenor, even the alto, as well as some instrumentalists, particularly two violists, had been granted a scholarship by the Respected and Honourable Council, and thus had been motivated to reinforce church music.

The present situation of music has completely changed since that time, the art of music has improved, tastes have changed remarkably, and the kind of music which had been played at the time, no longer sounds good to our ears. Therefore, substantial means would be necessary to choose and appoint musicians who satisfy the present musical taste playing the new sorts of music and are able to do justice to the composer and his work. However, the low allowances to the choirs have not been increased as necessary, but instead have been reduced and totally ceased. It is very peculiar that German musicians are expected to be able to play all sorts of music, whether it come from Italy or France, from England or Poland, just like that without preparation, like those virtuosos for whom this music has been written and who have studied it a long time, until they almost know it by heart and besides, what must not be forgotten, receive an appropriate income for their work. However, things like that are not taken into account at all. The musicians are left alone with their worries; due to their problems earning their living elsewhere, some of them cannot even think of practising to become perfect or distinguish themselves. As an example I only have to mention the court of Dresden, where His Royal Majesty pays the musicians remarkable salaries. Since those musicians do not have to worry how they should earn their living, and thus can live happy and carefree lives, and since each person only has to play a single instrument, the music they perform must consequently sound wonderful and excellent. Accordingly, it is clear that I am deprived of any means to improve the music in our churches, if my allowances continue to be reduced.

Finally, I feel forced to mention the pupils by name and assess their musical talent. It has to be carefully considered if under these circumstances, music can continue to exist, or if it will deteriorate even more. But it is necessary to divide all the pupils into three groups.

The following can be employed:

1. Pezold, Lange and Stoll as prefects. Frick, Krause, Kittler, Pohlreuter, Stein, Bruckhard, Siegler, Nitzer, Reichhard, Krebs junior and senior, Schöneman, Heder and Dietel.

The motet singers who must first practise in order to be employed as figural singers are as follows:

2. Jänigke, Ludewig junior and senior, Meißner, Neucke senior and junior, Hillmeyer, Steidel, Hesse, Haupt, Suppius, Segnitz, Thieme, Keller, Röder, Ossan, Berger, Lösch, Hauptmann and Sachse.

The third group are pupils who are not talented at all in music. Their names are:

3. Bauer, Grass, Eberhard, Braune, Seyman, Tietze, Hebenstreit, Wintzer, Össer, Leppert, Haussius, Feller, Crell, Zeymer, Guffer, Eichel and Zwicker.

To sum up, it can be said that 17 of them can be employed, 20 cannot yet be employed, and 17 cannot be employed at all.

Leipzig, August 23, 1730.

Joh. Seb. Bach.

Musical Director.

Johann Matthias Gesner described Bach's work with the musicians in 1738. He did so in the form of a Latin reference note to a text by the Roman poet Quintilian. In translation, it reads:

You would call all of this irrelevant, Fabius, if you came back from Hades and could see Bach – to mention him as an example – who was my colleague at St. Thomas's school in Leipzig only some years ago. The way he can play the clavier for instance, which alone comprises many kitharas, with both hands and all of his fingers, or that basic instrument whose numerous pipes are blown by bellows – how he hurries over the keys, here with both hands, there with quick feet, and produces veritable armies of very different but still matching notes. If you could see him and listen to his recitals, several of your kitharists and numerous flautists could not perform; how he not only sings a melody like the kithara singer, and keeps his own part, but at the same time supervises all of his 30 or even 40 musicians and makes them keep time and rhythm by nodding his head, by stamping his foot, or by lifting his finger threateningly; how he gives the note – high, deep or medium – to each of them. How in the middle of the loudest performance by the musicians, although he himself has the most difficult part, he immediately realizes if anything is not as it should be; how he keeps them all together and remedies any problems and brings back security if there is any insecurity; how he feels time in all his body, controls the harmonies with a good ear and brings forth all the voices with his own limited throat. In other respects, I am an enthusiastic adorer of Antiquity, but I believe that my friend Bach alone and anyone similar to him is several times better than Orpheus and twenty times better than Arion.

117. Autograph: Title page of the St. Matthew Passion.

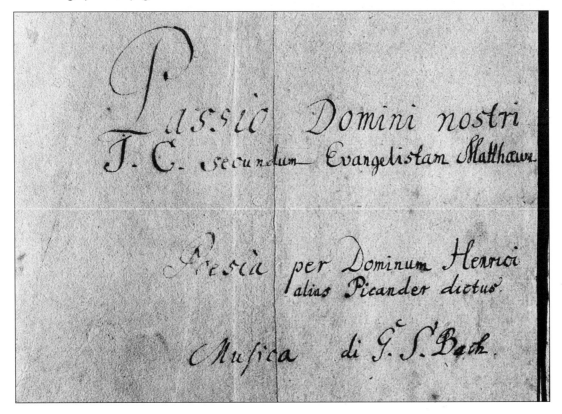

118. Salomon Deyling (1677-1755). Engraving.

Here we see a portrait of a perfectionist obsessed with music. Similar words could be used to describe an excellent conductor who plays his own instrument in the orchestra. However, he would have to be his own composer and not an interpreter of Bach's music. Gesner had had the opportunity to watch Bach for four years, and he wrote down his impressions with the hindsight of some years. These circumstances make his description credible. However, we must not overesti-

mate the quality Bach achieved with his interpreters. Surviving manuscripts indicate that the copyists often – probably in most cases – did not finish copying the parts until shortly before the performances began. Long and thorough rehearsals were impossible. They may have been possible for special occasions, such as for the performance of the Passions. However, most performances were probably only preceded by making arrangements. Many mistakes by the copyists are still to be seen in the individual sheets of music – missing markings and bar-lines, which would have been corrected or added during thorough rehearsal – and lead us to assume that there was sometimes no time at all for rehearsals. If performances sometimes had to take place without rehearsal – which is quite possible – the paramount skill of the musical director, described by Gesner, was even more important. This was the only way to avoid bad mistakes by singers and instrumentalists. When cantatas whose parts had been finished before were repeated, some improvised original performance may have been improved and may have become precise interpretations.

During his first years in Leipzig, Bach only performed his own cantatas in the two principal churches. In practice, this meant that he had to compose a new cantata, lasting some 20 to 30 minutes every week, write down the voice parts – with the assistance of family members and elder pupils – and rehearse the new cantata for performance on the Sunday or festival day. Only rarely was Bach able to use cantatas he had written during his time at Weimar. In later years, he increasingly used works by other composers, but in the services at the main churches, he predominantly played his own cantatas. The period when he created cantatas in Leipzig was limited to his first decade in the city, and within this period to the first five years. The reader who wants more detailed information on the cantatas is recommended to read Alfred Dürr's extensive book on them, which lists those he composed in Leipzig in each period. Let us follow him in our short survey. The origin of the texts listed in the first period, the years 1723 and 1724, is still obscure. Only one cantata, 'Ein ungefärbt Gemüt' (A pure mind; BWV 24), can be ascribed to a librettist – Erdmann Neumeister. Cantatas composed by Bach at Weimar to texts by Luther, Franck, Neumeister and Lehms were added to the

ecclesiastical year in Leipzig without revision. As early as this first period, several pastiches can be found: Bach used compositions or parts of compositions from earlier years with new texts. During his years in Leipzig, he repeatedly added parts of secular cantatas to the church cantatas. On Trinity Sunday, two-part cantatas were predominant. Sometimes Bach seems to have given recitals of two one-part cantatas instead of one consisting of two parts in one service.

In the second period, dating from 1724 to 1725, Bach followed an old Leipzig tradition. He used Pietist hymns whose texts he revised himself or had revised. The introductory and final movements mostly corresponded to the texts and music of the old hymns. Then Bach composed nine cantatas to texts by the Leipzig librettist Christiane Mariane von Ziegler. Here again he revised the texts whenever he considered it necessary for his music. Particularly in the period between Easter and Pentecost, he often used pastiches. Probably Bach had so much work due to the composition and rehearsal of the Passions, which took much more time than normal cantatas, and due to the many festival days between the week before Easter and Pentecost, that he hardly had time to compose completely new cantatas. Some of the oratorios also came into being at this time of year.

The third Leipzig period lasted from 1725 to 1727. As Alfred Dürr says in his summary, this period:

. . . was no longer the result of continual compositions of cantatas finished within a year. Either the cantatas that have been preserved are a mixture of two years (strictly speaking of three years if the adapted cantatas from period II are added), or Bach took a break in the time after the Trinity Sunday of 1725, which could be the reason for the extension of the following period.

In 1728, Picander also became prominent

uë près de la Porte dit Thomas-Pforte, à Leipzig. | *Prospect bey der Thomas-Pforte, zu Leipzig.*

119. The rear elevation of St. Thomas's church and school with St. Thomas's gate. Coloured Engraving by Georg Balthasar Probst, 1762.

as librettist for Bach's sacred cantatas. As early as 1725, he wrote the text for a cantata on the occasion of the birthday of Duke Christian of Saxe-Weissenfels. The texts of the St. Matthew Passion and the lost St. Mark Passion were written by him, as perhaps were those of the Christmas and Easter Oratorios. Although Picander was a mediocre poet, he had two ideal qualities for writing the libretti for Bach's compositions: he was a musician himself and knew how to adapt his texts perfectly to Bach's musical wishes, and he was also a master at writing texts to compositions which already existed. Bach, who constantly had a very heavy load of work in his first decade in Leipzig, greatly appreciated this ability in Picander. An entire year of cantatas whose texts had been published by Picander in 1728 entitled '*Cantatas for the Sundays and Festival Days Through the Entire Year*', with a note that they had been set to music by Bach, has been lost except for a few sheets of music by Bach and some copies.

From the time after 1728, only a few sacred

169

120. The New Church. Engraving after Joachim Ernst Scheffler, 1749.

121. The church of St. Peter and St. Peter's gate. Engraving after J. E. Scheffler, 1749.

122. Autograph MS of the cantata *'Nun komm, der Heiden Heiland'* (Now come, Saviour of the heathen; BWV 61). On the back of the title page, Bach noted the liturgy at Leipzig.

123. Conductor.

124. Trumpeter.

125. Clarinet

126. Viola d'amore.

127. Oboe

128. Violin or viola.

129. Conductor and orchestra.

Musicians of Bach's time and their instruments. Engraving of the 'Musical Theatre' by Johann Christian Weigel, 1722.

130. Viola da gamba.

131. Bass flute.

cantatas by Bach are extant. By that time he had enough material to be able to perform his service in church as a Cantor. Since each cantata had to correspond to the respective part of the Gospel, these themes of the ecclesiastical year had more or less been exhausted by Bach; only someone writing mass-produced articles could have composed more and more cantatas on the same themes. Bach, however, preferred to improve existing works, or revise compositions by others. In spite of the richness of ideas and forms he possessed, he certainly became tired and exhausted. He was in his mid forties by this time. External difficulties in his office at the church increased. In 1726, he had begun to publish his 'Clavier Exercise' consisting of several parts. When he took over the musical college in 1729, the composer and musical director Bach faced new musical tasks. He directed this group of musicians – with an interruption of two years – for almost one and a half decades. With this group, he entertained the inhabitants of Leipzig with a musical evening every week in his favourite café, 'Zimmermann's Coffee House.' These performances of secular music with the students was certainly a welcome change from the Cantor's frequent problems in his church job, particularly in summer when they could take place in the café garden.

In the following years, Bach mostly added to existing cantatas and revised for the ecclesiastical year compositions he had written for weddings, birthdays and funerals. In his passions he had already abandoned the restraints of the Sunday cantatas. In the years 1734 and 1735, he turned to new forms in his oratorios. In these pieces that – in contrast to the cantatas – followed a plot from the Bible, he used many passages from earlier compositions, revising them and composing new parts. Dürr writes:

In the year 1735 – 15 years before his death – the development of Bach's church cantatas was completed; the few works he composed in later years did not add anything new to the proud and manifold history of this genre. Although church cantatas were to be played and developed further in the second half of the century, they lost their prominence among musical genres. They flourished in obscurity, as the creation of minor composers, and none of the great masters to come would be able to say that his ultimate aim was 'a well-regulated church music for God's honour'.

This development of a new era with a different understanding of music began while the aged Bach continued to serve as Cantor of St. Thomas's for many years. This was no longer his era. He was already on his way to the 'Art of the Fugue,' ahead of his time. Although he never once thought that his music might become important for posterity, but thought only of his God, he sorted out many of his manuscripts and corrected them. He did not want to leave anything looking as if it could be improved. Perhaps he even thought that one manuscript or another of his works could be of use for some other musicians beside himself – perhaps for his sons, of whom only Carl Philipp Emanuel seems to have had any idea of his father's greatness. But how could his contemporaries be expected to understand his genius, if he himself did not have the least idea of the importance he would attain in later years? Neither did he have any time for ideas like that. *I had to work hard; those who work as hard as I did will achieve the same,* he is said to have said. Friedrich Schiller's phrase two generations later – 'genius means industriousness' – could have derived from studying Bach.

132. In Leipzig, no original organ dating from Bach's time has been preserved, but there is one in the little town of Rötha, ten miles (15 kilometres) away from the city. Probably Bach also played this organ built by Silbermann.

SDG: Soli Deo Gloria

'SDG' – *Soli Deo Gloria* (for the glory of God alone) – is written at the end of many partitas by Bach; and at their beginning, we can read: 'JJ' – (*Jesu juva*; Jesus help). As a faithful Lutheran Christian, Bach shared a heartfelt joy in this life. Throughout his life, hours of secular happiness, even carefree joy, contradicted his almost mystical longing for death and salvation. This longing became particularly visible in his cantatas: '*Liebster Gott, wann werd ich sterben*' (Dearest God, when will I die), '*Was frag ich nach der Welt*' (Why should I ask for the world), '*Komm, du süße Todesstunde*' (Come, sweet hour of death). Such and similar are the titles of many cantatas. Bach believed in salvation and life after death. The promise of eternal life after his earthly wandering reconciled Bach to all the burdens, pains and struggles for survival in this world, which he accepted with a deep confidence in God. If his music can be explained at all, then the explanation must lie in this basic attitude of the mystic towards life and death. The richness of his musical forms cannot ultimately be analyzed with the intellect alone. For the mystic, spirit and form were a unit. It is possible to admire and interpret Bach's works from a musical, aesthetic point of view. But then only part of his music is touched. According to a record by one of Bach's pupils, Bach demanded in his teaching about the basso continuo:

In the end, also the aim or final purpose of all the music and as such also of the basso continuo is to be only for the glory of God and the soul's enjoyment. Wherever this is not taken into consideration, there cannot really be music.

Aesthetics is also a question of philosophy of life and thus of faith. We only need to compare Albrecht Dürer's apocalypse to the visions of doom by many artists of our time. The reason for this difference is certainly not a change of reality. Our ancestors were just as afraid of the Last Judgement as we and our contemporaries are of an atomic inferno. But there is a decisive difference: for the faithful Christian who waits for the end of the earth, whenever its last hour may come, man is not the measure of all things. He knows that in his activity and creativity as well as in his errors and sins, he will be responsible to somebody who is higher than he. For this reason, Dürer was able to create his frightening apocalypse humbly before God in an aesthetically beautiful form. And for the same reason, Bach was able to express the pain and suffering of this world in such a wonderful way in his cantatas and passions two centuries later. Faithful humility creates its own form, just as atheistic arrogance perverts and destroys it. Throughout the history of civilization, faith in God united with a longing for form, harmony and aesthetics, if it did not degenerate and become heretical through fanaticism and intolerance. It is only a logical consequence that materialism and the emancipation of the human mind which is no longer subordinated to any religious and ethical self-control leads to ugliness, formlessness and ultimately to contempt for humanity. But the distorted picture of this other world,

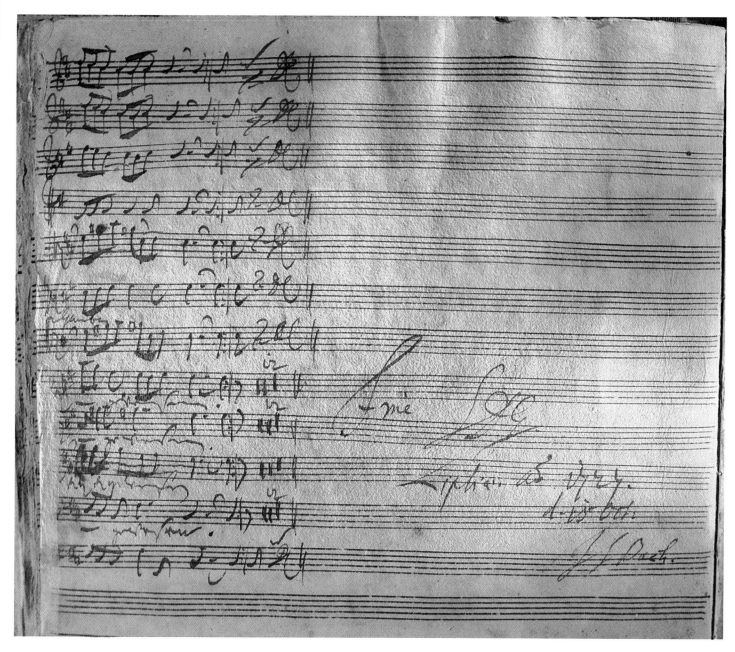

133. The end of the cantata 'Lass, Fürstin, lass noch einen Strahl' (BWV 198)
with Bach's signature 'Fine SDG'

contradictory to Bach's understanding of the world and of art, is probably declining. Many people, particularly the young, are looking for new directions, for a rock amidst the turmoil of the times. And here is this court Kapellmeister and Cantor Bach with his music. He did not change anything intellectually in the great 'Enlightenment' that began changing Europe while he was still alive. He never overestimated his intellect. But his music reached far beyond his time, as did the great cathedrals of the past. It reveals a balance of emotion and spirit that no other master of the art of music has achieved before or since. In its elemental nature, this music tells of a humane world with faith in God. 'Soli Deo Gloria.'

If we compare his letters and documents to those of his scholarly contemporaries or of his sons, Bach was less 'educated' than they

177

134. Giovanni Pierluigi Palestrina (1525-1594). Engraving.

works are still admired today aspired to be. When he used music by other masters for carrying out his duties in Leipzig or any-where else in his musical life, he did so 'SDG.' They all tried to glorify Almighty God with their music, although they were sinners just as we are. The fact that no copyright existed at the time was not the only reason why musicians copied from one another without scruples. Can we imagine Georg Frideric Handel suing Bach for copying and performing his Brockes Passion? Thus, the two greatest composers of their time, who were born in the same year, at least met in their music manuscripts (illness prevented Bach from meeting Handel personally when the latter visited his native town of Halle). Works by Frescobaldi, Palestrina, Conti, Caldara, Telemann, Vivaldi and others were copied, shortened or lengthened by Bach, or their instrumentation changed; they were not regarded as the individual property of their composers, in the way they would be today

135. Antonio Caldara (1670-1736). Drawing by Theodor Schmidtlein.

were. He was no scholar. Rector Ernesti's words were much more polished and logical than Bach's. Some court or town clerk had more refined arguments than the man who composed the St. Matthew Passion, the B minor Mass and the 'Art of the Fugue.' The question arises: What is really important in art? Education and intellect alone are certainly not. Otherwise many educated composers of later times would not have looked insignificant in the shadow of this uneducated Cantor of St. Thomas's, Johann Sebastian Bach. He would probably have refused to be referred to as a 'genius' or as the 'creator' of music – attributes posterity has bestowed on him. He considered himself a servant, and a servant he was, primarily, a servant of God. That was what all of those whose musical

136. Georg Frideric Handel (1685-1759). Oil painting by Thomas Hudson, 1748.

178

by companies, managers and lawyers. They were common property and ultimately all belonged to the one to whom they were dedicated: God.

Bach's works mark the peak of an era that considered an artist to be a craftsman who used his mind. The term 'genius' as it was used in the 19th century did not yet exist. Singing and making music were an indispensable part of everyday life, just as familiar to people as driving a car or watching TV are today. Music was what contemporaries wrote on sheets of music and played, or often improvised. Few printed editions or copies of compositions by previous masters supplemented the manuscript material. Not until a century later did people begin to study the works from the past, systematically researching and cultivating them. Artists still lived and worked together with their contemporaries, and not in opposition to them. Bach united everyday life and creativity more harmoniously than most personalities in the history of music. Bach never knew the bitter and humiliating struggle with ignorant contemporaries that Mozart or Schubert had to endure two generations later. He worked in harmony with the people of his time. Events and persons nobody would remember today are known to later generations only because he dedicated compositions to them. The people Bach complimented in this way rewarded him with money or esteem – in most cases both. This is true of princes and burghers, of town councils and of musical institutions. Nobody would ever refer to the *Corresponding Society of Musical Sciences* of Leipzig, a group of musicians founded in 1738 by Lorenz Christoph Mizler, if Bach had not become its 14th member in July 1748. The rules demanded that the society sent compositions by its members *every Easter and Michaelmas in a package to all the members to ask for their impartial opinion.* Thus, Mizler's Society (as it was named after its founder) also distributed compositions Bach had written in the last years of his life. Thanks to this society, we even know what Bach looked like when he was old. According to section 21 of the society's rules, each new member had to present a painting and a composition. For this purpose, Bach appears to have had himself painted by the Saxon court painter and painter of the Leipzig council, Elias Gottlob Haussmann. In his right hand, he holds the manuscript of the

137. Bach's copy of the Brockes Passion by Georg Frideric Handel.

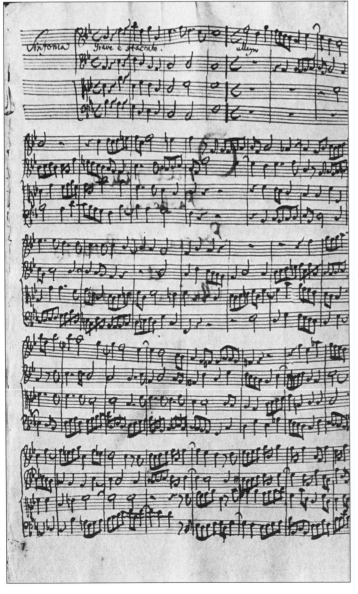

138. Antonio Vivaldi (1678-1741). Oil painting.

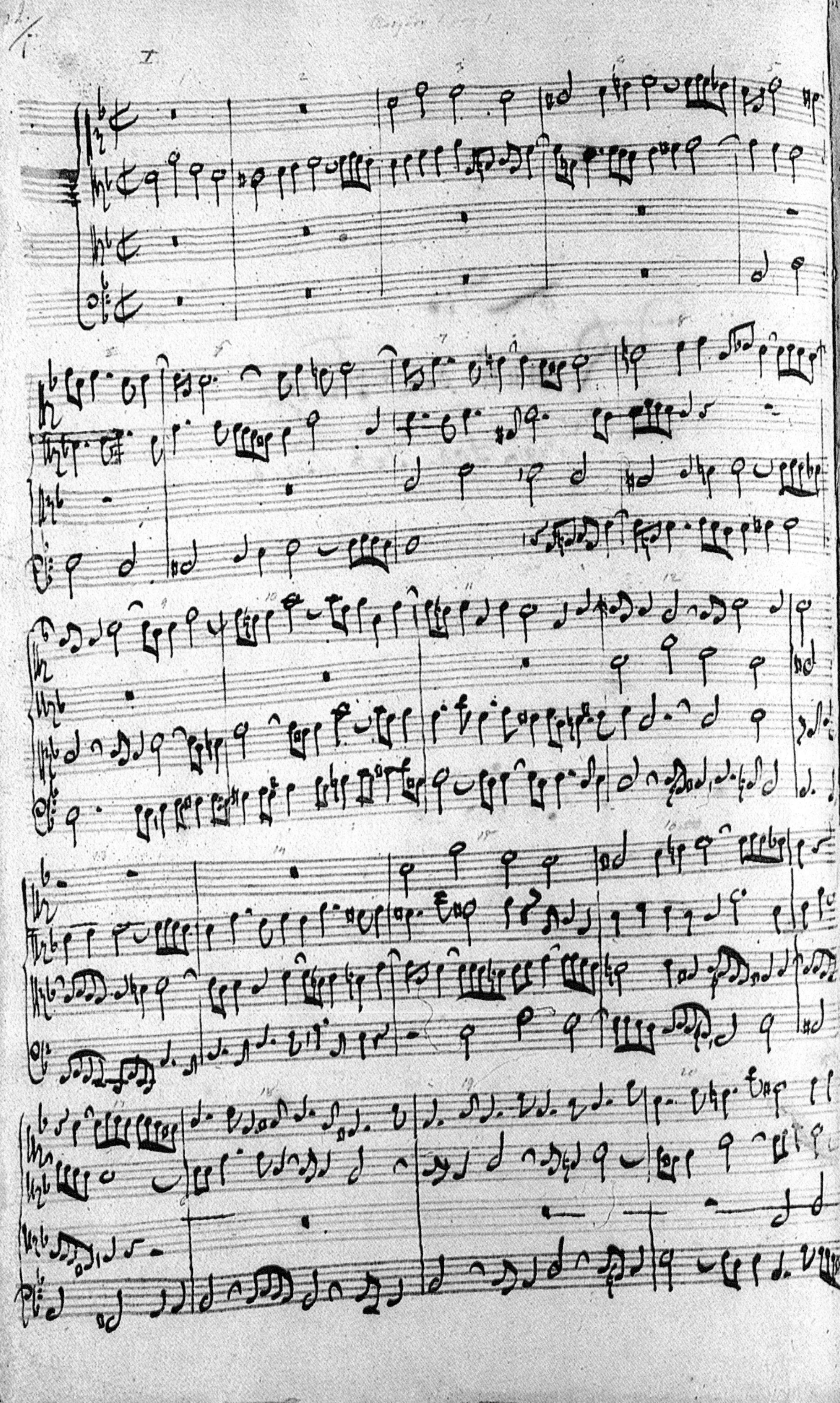

'Rätselkanon' (puzzle canon; BWV 1076) that he presented to the society when he became a member. This painting by Haussmann is the only extant portrait of Bach which is absolutely authenticated. Haussmann himself copied it later. At the same time it was a model for numerous other portraits of Bach. Since Haussmann was a good painter, we can assume that Bach really looked like this portrait in the last years of his life.

The eye problems he suffered from at the end of his life cannot be seen on this portrait. But even if symptoms were visible, the painter certainly would not have painted them in his picture. Bach, who had been extraordinarily healthy throughout his life, became extremely short-sighted in his old age – doubtless partly a consequence of writing many manuscripts without sufficient light. He probably suffered from cataracts at the end of his life. A famous English eye specialist, John Taylor, came to Leipzig at the end of March 1750. Bach underwent eye surgery by this specialist twice, but to no avail. This is documented in a report by a Leipzig physician dated May 1750. However, it was not published until two years after Bach's death:

Here is a detailed and impartial report about the patient operated on by the Chevalier Taylor. For whenever I met people with a black bandage over their eyes who had been operated on by him, I asked how they were. Many of them, however, have not yet been seen. Among them is Mr B—, whose cataract has been operated on. Several days later, public papers wrote that he could see perfectly again. But this patient again lost his eyesight, because the cataract returned, and underwent surgery a second time and repeatedly suffered from inflammations and other problems.

At the end of his life, Bach worked on a task the Bach specialist Werner Neumann called *an immense monument to polyphonic music, 'The Art of the Fugue'* (BWV 1080). It starts out with the *Simple Fugue about the Theme in its Basic Form* and consists in its entirety of 14 fugues and four canons on this single theme. All imaginable types of fugues are designed around this single theme. Such a complex and technical musical structure might be expected to drown any natural melodic flow. But Bach's richness of invention, his inexhaustible musical ideas, always produce a completely natural sound that makes the listener forget any theories about the complex structure. In the *'Art of the Fugue,'* Bach again summed up all his musical thinking and feeling. It is Bach's last masterpiece, in which at the end of his life he achieved perfect unity of form and content.

On July 22, 1750, Bach took communion at St. Thomas's church for the last time. A stroke, followed by high fever, put an end to his life. Carl Philipp Emanuel reported that his father *died quietly and peacefully at the age of 66 on the evening of July 28, 1750, at 9.15, despite every possible treatment by two of the most capable doctors of Leipzig.* Bach's body was buried in the cemetery of St. John's church in Leipzig. Some years later his grave fell into oblivion. Towards the end of the 19th century, his mortal remains were searched for to bring them to a more respected place. But by then, Johann Sebastian Bach had long since entered into another life. On earth too his music had been rediscovered.

139. Autograph MS of the 'Art of the Fugue.'

Appendix
Literature and References

The author's intention has been to paint a picture of Bach's life and personality for lovers of Johann Sebastian Bach's music, using those documents which researchers have so far authenticated. Studying secondary literature is one of the indispensable preconditions of such a work. However, I do not mean to pretend I have studied all the enormous number of books that have been published since Johann Nikolaus Forkel's first biography of Bach in 1802. The number of books not only about Bach's compositions, but also about his personality has grown immensely since Forkel. It is necessary to be selective.

The authors of books about Bach – as might be expected – differ both over basic issues and over many details of Bach's life and legacy. This discussion of different opinions is necessary, often fruitful and almost always stimulating – even in those areas where the reader disagrees with the theories put forward. But I do not want to deal with such controversial interpretations of Bach and his music in this book. It seems to me that the large and ever-growing audience for Bach's music will not get acquainted with Bach by reading discussions in popular books if Bach's life and work are considered in a way that is too theological, atheistic, denominational, Marxist, nationalist and so forth. There is no apologist who knows everything and interprets everything without error; this is even more impossible with the personality and the work of a great man who lived two and a half centuries ago. By focusing on

Bach's own documents and the witness of his contemporaries, I avoided this dilemma of all secondary literature, including that about Bach.

Thus, the four supplementary volumes of the *Neue Ausgabe Sämtlicher Werke* by Johann Sebastian Bach formed the basis of my work. They were published under the collective title of *Bach-Dokumente* between 1963 and 1979 by the Bach Archives of Leipzig, and have been published, as mentioned in the preface, by Bärenreiter and VEB Deutscher Verlag für Musik. To date, they are the most extensive collection of documents of all kinds about Bach's music and personality. Volume I contains documents in Bach's own hand, edited and annotated by Werner Neumann and Hans-Joachim Schulze. Volume II, edited by the same authors, comprises documents written by others or printed documents about Bach's life up to his death. Volume III, edited and annotated by Hans-Joachim Schulze, includes documents about Bach from 1750 to 1800 and is also of great importance for anyone who wants to study Bach's life and work. Although the documents of this volume were written after Bach's death, there are many first-hand testimonies, documents by Bach's son, Carl Philipp Emanuel, by his friends and contemporaries. Volume IV finally is an extensive collection of pictures, presented by Werner Neumann, who was director of the Bach Archives in Leipzig for many years. It contains 54 photographs, with comments about the history of each picture of Bach, from the first portrait painted by Haussmann to the disputed portraits from his youth and the numerous posthumous pictures of Bach. The 623 pictures about Bach's life and their explanations also contain much information. Unfortunately, the technical standard of the photography and printing is poor, but this does not reduce the value of this fourth supplementary volume.

Besides the supplementary volumes, I still consider Albert Schweitzer's book *Johann Sebastian Bach* (first German edition 1908) a fundamental work about Bach and his music. The value of this book is not diminished by the fact that some details have since been added or corrected by researchers. The eleventh edition of Schweitzer's book is published by Breitkopf & Härtel. Albert Schweitzer was a great organist, philosopher and theologian, one of the universal humanistic personalities of the twentieth century. Many of his thoughts and insights are timeless. Alfred Dürr's book *Die Kantaten von Johann Sebastian Bach* has been referred to several times in this book. It too was very important for my own work.

There is not enough room in this epilogue to mention all the musicians who helped me understand Bach's music over the course of the years, not only by interpreting it but also by explaining it. I am thankful to all of them, as well as to all the scientists whose efforts and achievements form the basis of our present knowledge about Bach and his music. Whenever I came across factual questions during my work, I could call Dr Klaus Hofmann to whom I am particularly grateful for his helpfulness. He is director of the

Johann Sebastian Bach Institute at Göttingen that edited the *Neue Ausgabe Sämtlicher Werke* by Johann Sebastian Bach in a co-edition with the Bach Archives in Leipzig.

This book was written in 1984 and first published in 1985. The references below refer to that time. My book was preceded by my full-length film *Johann Sebastian Bach*. For this film, I studied Bach's music and life closely for two years – from the first sketch of the script until the entire film was finished in both German and English. Of course, many insights and much information learned during this period can be found in this book. The film was a co-production by ORF (Austrian Television), DDR-F (Television of the German Democratic Republic) and FFF (Fischer Film and TV production) and is also available on videocassettes. When writing and producing this film, I received much help from many cultural institutions and churches in the divided Germany. I also want to express my thanks to them here. It was very important for my knowledge of Bach and thus for the present book to have the chance to visit all the places of Bach's life and work and to be able to study many important original documents such as autograph manuscripts, historical files and pictures.

I want to thank all my colleagues who helped me write this book. With regard to this dimension of the life and work of Johann Sebastian Bach, it would be ridiculous to think a single book about Bach could be more than a little piece in the huge mosaic of thoughts people will continue to design as long as there will be music.

The Pictures in this Book

In the 19th century, most of the extant music autograph MSS by Bach as well as the copies by Anna Magdalena were gathered from various collections and brought to the Royal Library in Berlin, which was later called the National Library of Prussia; today it is called the German National Library, Berlin. After the first heavy bomb attack on Berlin in 1941, it was decided to conceal the valuable collection of autograph MSS of the National Library of Prussia somewhere outside Berlin. The major portion went to Grüssau, which belonged to Silesia at the time, others to western Germany. This decision to move the collection probably saved the autograph MSS.

After the war, those autographs which had been hidden in the eastern parts of former Germany returned for the most part to the (East) German National Library, Berlin. The manuscripts that had been hidden in West Germany first remained in Marburg or Tübingen, before being moved to the National Library of Prussian Culture in (West) Berlin. Thus, while I was working on this book, Bach's legacy was split up; today it has been re-united. Some autographs are private property and scattered all over the world.

I am very grateful to the music departments of the German National Library, Berlin (former DDR) and of the National Library of Prussian Culture (former West Berlin) – today united as the National Library of Berlin-Prussian Culture – for their assistance. All the music manuscripts of Bach illustrated in this book were at that time available in the two libraries in Berlin, which were only a few hundred metres apart, but separated by the Berlin Wall. (An exception to this is Bach's alto for the B minor Mass, which was reproduced in a facsimile edition by Hänssler-Verlag in 1983. The original MSS are kept in the National Library of Saxony, in Dresden.)

The letters and other documents written by Bach are to be found in several archives in Germany. Few of them are in other countries. Bach's most important extant letter, the one to Georg Erdmann, is in the Central National History Archives in Moscow and has been reproduced in facsimile.

Most of the pictures reproduced about the history of Bach's life – pictures and documents about his contemporaries, the towns and places where he lived and worked etc. – were kept in the German National Library of Berlin, the Museum of History of the city of Leipzig, the National Bach Institutes (former DDR) and in the Bach Archives of Leipzig in which the National Bach Institutes were united after German reunification, further in the so-called 'Bach House' at Eisenach as well as in the city archives and Music Library of the city of Leipzig, in the museum at Cöthen and in the Museum of the History of Hamburg. I am grateful to all those institutions, as well as to the churches of St. Thomas's, Leipzig; St. John's, Lüneburg; St. James's, Hamburg and to the office of the superintendent of Mühlhausen and the presbytery of Gehren in Thuringia.

The original paintings of Dresden, and of the electoral princes of Saxony and Electoral Princess Maria Josepha are part of the rich property of the National Art Gallery of Dresden. The painting of the young Prussian king, Frederick II, is the property of the National Castles and Gardens of Potsdam-Sanssouci, the historic pictures of Weimar and its dukes are in the Art Gallery of Weimar and in the National Institute and Museum of German Classics at Weimar. I am grateful to all these national institutions.

Copies of a number of historic pictures presented in this book, such as Merian copperplates and lithographs of towns, are held in several museums and libraries. I have tried to use the best of these pictures. To describe each source in detail would go beyond the scope of this book, which is not primarily written for scholars. I am sure that the respective institutions and private owners who allowed me to use their pictures will accept my deep gratitude in this form.

Bach's legacy and the texts and pictures about his life – not only those reproduced in this book, of course – are for the most part today scattered among several museums, libraries and archives in Germany. Some valuable documents are in other European countries and in the USA. Everywhere Bach specialists work with love and expertise to preserve the precious historic materials which have survived the destruction of two World Wars and must be preserved for later generations. While working on my film and on my book about Bach some years before the reunification of the two German states, I experienced the preservation of Bach's legacy as an example of positive cultural activity and co-existence despite political differences between both German states. Bach's works and his personality are today the property of the entire world. They encourage all of us to commit ourselves to humanity. Only in a peaceful world can the great values of culture survive.

I am especially grateful to Michael Epp for his photographic assistance. The pictures in this book have been reproduced from our own photographs, except for the following pictures: no. 5 – photo by Ingrid Trautmann; nos. 47, 48 – German National Library, Berlin; no. 136 – National Portrait Gallery, London; no. 138 – Civico Museo Musicale, Bologna.

INDEX

The numbers in this index refer to the pages in the text, the numbers in italics refer to the numbers of the pictures and captions. The name of Johann Sebastian Bach has been omitted in this index.

INDEX OF NAMES

INDEX OF TOWNS AND CITIES

A musical journey through the life of Johann Sebastian Bach

1. Ohrdruf, Lüneburg, Arnstadt
(1696–1707)

1. Capriccio sopra la lontananza del fratello dilettissimo

BWV 992 (DATING FROM 1705 ?)   03:45   VOL.102

Aria di Postiglione
Fuga all'imitatione di Posta

Robert Hill, Harpsichord

Fig. 12: St. Michael's church, Ohrdruf

2. Toccata and Fugue in D Minor

BWV 565 (DATING FROM 1708?)   08:30   VOL. 89

Kay Johannsen,
Arp Schnitger-Organ, Cappel

Figs. 15 & 24: Organs in Lüneburg and Arnstadt;
No. 20: Arnstadt

2. Mühlhausen (1707–1708)

3. Cantata "Gott ist mein König"

BWV 71 (1708)   01:50   VOL. 23

First movement:
Gott ist mein König von altersher

Gächinger Kantorei & Bach-
Collegium Stuttgart, Helmuth Rilling
Fig. 25: Mühlhausen in the 17th century

3. Weimar (1708–1717)

4. Toccata E Minor

BWV 914 (c. 1710)   03:30   VOL.104

IV: Fuga (Allegro)

Peter Watchorn, Harpsichord
(according to Johann Heinrich
Harraß, before 1714)

Fig. 34: Johann Sebastian Bach as concert-master in Weimar

5. Kyrie eleison – Christe, du Lamm Gottes

BWV 233A (1708–1717)   03:40   VOL. 71

Gächinger Kantorei & Bach-
Collegium Stuttgart, Helmuth Rilling
WORLD PREMIERE RECORDING

6. "Christ lag in Todesbanden" from Orgelbüchlein

BWV 625 (1713/15)   01:20   VOL. 94

Wolfgang Zerer,
Frans Caspar Schnitger-Organ,
Martinikerk, Groningen

Fig. 35: Weimar Castle Chapel, Bach's sphere of activity

4. Köthen
(1717–1723)

7. Brandenburg Concerto No. 2

BWV 1047 (DATING FROM 1721)   05:00   VOL. 126

1st movement (Allegro)

Oregon Bach Festival Chamber
Orchestra, Helmuth Rilling

Fig. 45: Hall of mirrors in Köthen Castle

8. Partita in B Minor for Violin solo

BWV 1002 (1720)   04:35   VOL.119

5. Sarabande, 6. Double

Dmitry Sitkovetsky, Violin

Figs. 50 & 51: Manuscript of the B-Minor Partita,
Sarabande and Double

9. Clavier-Büchlein for Wilhelm Friedemann Bach from 1720

03:15   VOL.137

Prelude in C Major BWV 846 &
C Minor BWV 847 (=The Well-
Tempered Clavier Part 1)

Joseph Payne,
Harpsichord & Clavichord

Fig. 90: Wilhelm Friedemann Bach

5. Leipzig (1723–1750)

10. St. John Passion

BWV 245 (1724)   08:30   VOL. 75

Opening chorus:
Herr, unser Herrscher

Gächinger Kantorei & Bach-
Collegium Stuttgart, Helmuth Rilling

Fig. 114: Church of St Nikolai at the time of Bach

11. Sonata for flute and basso continuo

BWV 1034 (1720-1724)   02:55   VOL.121

2nd movement: Allegro

Jean-Claude Gérard, Sergio Azzolini,
Boris Kleiner

12. St. Matthew Passion

BWV 244 (1727)   04:15   VOL. 74

Death scene: Und von der sechsten
Stunde – Wenn ich einmal soll
scheiden

Michael Schade, Matthias Goerne,
Gächinger Kantorei & Bach-
Collegium Stuttgart, Helmuth Rilling

Fig. 115: Manuscript of St. Matthew Passion, death scene

13. Prelude, Fugue and Allegro in E flat Major

(c. 1740)   03:30   VOL.109

III: Allegro

Robert Hill, Lute-harpsichord

Fig. 84: List of instruments bequeathed by J.S.Bach
No. 6: 1 lute mechanism

14. Musical Offering

BWV 1079 (1747)   02:31   VOL.133

Canons 1-3

Karl Kaiser, Flute; Gottfried von der
Goltz, Violin; Michael Behringer,
Harpsichord

Fig 110: King Frederick II of Prussia, known as Frederick the
Great, gave Bach the subject for the 'Musical Offering'.

15. The Art of Fugue

BWV 1080 (AFTER 1740/1750)   03:05   VOL.134

Contrapunctus I

Robert Hill, Harpsichord

Fig. 139: Manuscript of the "The Art of Fugue"

16. Organ chorale "Vor deinen Thron tret ich hiermit"

BWV 668 (AFTER 1740/1750?)   06:35   VOL.100

Martin Lücker, Rieger-Organ,
St. Katherine's Church,
Frankfurt am Main

17. Mass in B Minor

BWV 232 (c. 1748/49)   07:10   VOL. 70

Confiteor-Et expecto resurrectionem
mortuorum

Gächinger Kantorei & Bach-
Collegium Stuttgart, Helmuth Rilling

Figs. 123-131: The conductor and his orchestra

Extracts from the 172 CDs of
EDITION BACHAKADEMIE,
the first and only complete
recording of the music of
Johann Sebastian Bach.

Compilation by Dr. Andreas Bomba